Carl Sternheim

Twayne's World Authors Series

Ulrich Weisstein, Editor of German Literature

Indiana University

TWAS 671

Carl Sternheim

By Burghard Dedner
University of Marburg

Twayne Publishers · Boston

Carl Sternheim

Burghard Dedner

Copyright © 1982 by G. K. Hall & Company
All Rights Reserved
Published by Twayne Publishers
A Division of G. K. Hall & Company
70 Lincoln Street
Boston, Massachusetts 02111

Book production by Marne B. Sultz
Book design by Barbara Anderson

Printed on permanent/durable acid-free
paper and bound in The United States of America.

German quotations reprinted by permission of
Luchterhand Verlag (Darmstadt) and English
quotations reprinted by permission of Calder &
Boyers (London) from the plays, *The Bloomers,
Paul Schippel Esq., The Snob, 1913*, and *The Fossil.*

Library of Congress Cataloging in Publication Data

Dedner, Burghard.
  Carl Sternheim.

  (Twayne's world authors series;
  TWAS 671)
  Bibliography: p. 163
  Includes index.
  1. Sternheim, Carl, 1878–1942
—Criticism and interpretation.
I. Title. II. Series
PT2639.T5Z62   1982   832'.912   82-8454
ISBN 0-8057-6518-2

For D.G.E.S.D.

Contents

About the Author

The author was born in 1942 in Berlin. He attended the universities of Berlin, Aix-en-Provence, and Tuebingen, from which he received his Ph.D. in 1968. He taught at Vassar College, the University of Giessen, and Indiana University, and is now professor of German at the University of Marburg (Germany). He has published *Topos, Ideal und Realitätstpostulat* (Tuebingen: Niemeyer, 1968) and articles on eighteenth- and twentieth-century German literature.

Preface

Prefaces to literary monographs can scarcely do without a bit of advertising, and for the present volume, part of a series concerned with world authors, such advertising may be even more necessary than usual. Is Carl Sternheim, one might well ask, a world author? If so, he is one whose fame has as yet scarcely spread beyond the borders of his own country. During his life (1878–1942) only three of his plays were performed abroad,[1] and two recent attempts to introduce him to the English stage[2] have not met with apparent success.

Within the German-speaking countries this situation is radically different. Between 1911 and 1925, Sternheim was hailed as the German Molière, and from 1960 on, after an intervening period in which his plays were either banned or rarely staged, his comedies have experienced a veritable renaissance.[3] There can be no doubt today that, next to Gerhart Hauptmann and Bertolt Brecht, Sternheim is the most successful German playwright of the twentieth century. He is, at the same time, the most controversial one.

Sternheim's major plays are comedies, which means that they belong to a genre which occurs in at least two distinctly different forms. Comedy can be an instrument of social censorship or—in literary terms—of satire; and the laughter which it provokes can be an expression of derision and contempt. Comedy can also, however, be a stimulant of joy, triumph, and exuberance; it can invite the audience to laugh with, not at, the play's central figures; it can, in the words of the philosopher Hegel, demonstrate man's ability to experience "piggish delight."[4] Do Sternheim's plays—critics have asked—belong to the first, the censorial, or to the second, the anarchic, category?

To this day, no agreement has been reached on this crucial question. Some critics plausibly argue that Sternheim's comedies have survived because they expose the typical mentality of the German bourgeois of the Wilhelminian era and thus help to explain not only the characteristics of early twentieth-century imperialism but also the turns which the country took in 1914 and then again in 1933.[5] This line of interpretation has prevailed throughout the history of Sternheim criticism. Sternheim has, in other words, gained his reputation as a writer of social satire. A second group of critics, however, has concluded that, on the contrary, Sternheim confronts his audience not with objects of derision, but with positive heroes whose triumphs are to be shared and whose characters are to be emulated.[6] This second form of interpretation is strongly suggested by the author's declarations of intent. Throughout his life, although with increasing vehemence in his later years, Sternheim protested the prevailing satirical reception of his plays which, in his opinion, was symptomatic of his public's well-known authoritarian fixation. Partly in sympathy with the author's stand, partly in order to make possible a historical evaluation of his works, the present study tends to argue in favor of the nonsatirical, quasi-anarchistic intentions of Sternheim's plays.

Fortunately, an evaluation of Sternheim's major writings does not totally revolve around the above question. A majority of critics in both parties agree on at least two facts: Sternheim was an excellent observer of his contemporaries, their behavioral characteristics, their forms of interaction, their gestures, and, above all, their petty fantasies; he knew how to conform with the laws of theater and of the comic genre, a rare achievement indeed in a country whose literary tradition is so conspicuously void of stageable comedies. Taken together, the realistic and the theatrical qualities of Sternheim's works should be sufficient grounds for at least an honorary membership in the academy of world authors.

The present study is primarily devoted to the six plays—five comedies and one drama—which Sternheim wrote in the short period between 1910 and 1915. It is almost exclusively upon these plays that Sternheim's fame rests. Further consideration is given to a collection of novellas which Sternheim published during the years of World War I. These novellas had a considerable impact on German expressionist prose and even today deserve more attention and more critical acclaim than they have generally received. The rest of Sternheim's works—all written either before 1910 or after 1920—are of decidedly more limited interest in respect to their literary quality. They cannot, however, be passed over in silence. Their discussion provides at least a biographical framework for Sternheim's major writings and can give the reader a sense of historical direction.

Sternheim's writings fall in a period of history in which Germany underwent a series of dramatic and mostly catastrophic political and social changes. They are both reflections of this process and attempts to shape its course. Especially in his later years, Sternheim was a politically engaged author who openly sided with leftist anarchist groups.[7] While it is true that most of his writings from this period have fallen into obscurity, they still need to be considered here because their political and aesthetic tenets mark the implicit goal toward which Sternheim's works had been striving all along. Conversely, a discussion of Sternheim's early years and formative experiences helps to explain both the controversial nature of his plays and their theatrical qualities. For the society in which Sternheim grew up theater was more than a mere means of communication or artistic medium. It was also, and perhaps more importantly, an instrument of political stabilization. One of the characteristics of the Wilhelminian empire was its attempt to erect aesthetic facades, to give a quasi-theatrical structure to the interactions of its citizens and to turn such roles and skills as directing, acting, and observing into features of daily life. It is against this background that many of Sternheim's theatrical achievements can best be understood; it is from this source too, however, that some of the more irritating aspects of his works spring. In all phases of his life, as an unpromising young author, as the writer of highly successful comedies, and as a supporter of anarchistic groups, Sternheim remained strongly influenced by the dubious powers of Wilhelminian theatrical estheticism.[8]

Burghard Dedner

University of Marburg

Chronology

1914   Reinhardt stages *Der Snob*. During the war years most of
       Sternheim's plays are banned from the stage.

1915   *Der Kandidat* (adaptation of Flaubert's *Le Candidat*) is
       staged in Vienna. Publication of *1913* in *Die Weissen Blät-
       ter*.

1916   *Tabula Rasa*. Intervenes in support of Belgian citizens who
       are to be tried by German military courts.

1917   First contacts with Gottfried Benn and the stage director
       Gustav Hartung. Staging of the plays *Der Geizige* (an
       adaptation of Molière's *L'Avare*) and *Perleberg*.

1918   Series of articles on the German revolution. Sternheim's es-
       says and novellas are published in book form.

1919   Evicted from Belgium and moves to Switzerland. Staging
       of *1913*, *Die Marquise von Arcis*, and *Tabula Rasa*.

1920   Suffers a nervous breakdown. *Europa* and *Berlin oder Juste
       Milieu*.

1921   *Tasso oder Kunst des Juste Milieu* [Tasso or the art of the Juste
       Milieu]. *Der entfesselte Zeitgenosse* [The unchained contempo-
       rary] and *Manon Lescaut* are staged.

1922   Staging of *Der Nebbich*. Publishes a series of political and
       philosophical articles in *Die Aktion*.

1923   Moves to Dresden. Staging of *Das Fossil*.

1925   Staging of *Oscar Wilde*. Break with the Aktionskreis.

1926   *Lutetia. Die Schule von Uznach* [Uznach School] is staged.

1927   Thea Bauer divorces Sternheim.

1928   Institutionalized for almost a year.

1930   Marries Pamela Wedekind (divorced in 1934). Moves to
       Brussels. *John Pierpont Morgan*.

1933   Hitler regime outlaws Sternheim's works. Tries unsuccess-
       fully to establish contact with non-German publishers and
       stage directors. Recurring nervous breakdowns until his
       death.

1936   *Vorkriegseuropa* [Prewar Europe], an autobiography.

1942   Sternheim dies in Brussels on November 3.

Chapter One

The Formative Years

The Roots of Aesthetic Opposition

Born in 1878, Sternheim belongs to the generation of writers such as Heinrich and Thomas Mann, Hugo von Hofmannsthal, Rainer Maria Rilke and Hermann Hesse, who were all born during the 1870s.[1] Their early years fall within the Bismarck era, a period which, in many respects, can be considered the heyday of the German bourgeoisie. The newly founded Prusso-German empire, to be sure, had certain similarities to a police state; yet, its oppressiveness was mainly directed against socialist workers or so-called unruly elements. The years between 1873 and 1895, it is equally true, were a period of lasting economic depression. Poverty was common among the working classes, and bankruptcies were a frequent occurrence in the mid-seventies. Yet, here again, these were catastrophes which did not touch the prevailing sense of bourgeois security, the general pride in recent national accomplishments and the usual middle-class trust in the beneficial nature of moderate progress.

Consequently, the childhood recollections of this generation and its general view of history exhibit a touch of nostalgia. All the above-mentioned writers criticized the development which Germany took after the end of the Bismarck era; their critical attitude, however, was based not so much on political or social grounds, as on an intense feeling of aesthetic and psychological discontent which they expressed in their writings. Life had been better once, more secure, more rewarding, and, above all, aesthetically more attractive than it was ever again to be. They had—or so they imagined—still seen in their early lives quasi-heroic figures, men of a greater caliber than later periods were likely to produce. In Thomas Mann's novel *Buddenbrooks*, for example, it is the relic of older times, the family's grandfather, who provides the yardstick against which his insecure and inept heirs could be measured. More than anything else, Old Buddenbrook is an aesthetically conceived figure: he represents the harmony of all those spheres of life which later generations experience only in the form of autonomous and mutually exclusive fragments. Similarly, the hero of Rilke's novel *Malte Laurids Brigge* had to go back to the generation of his grandparents to demonstrate that men were once able, if not to live their own lives, then at least to die their own deaths.

Sternheim's "nostalgia" follows much the same lines. In practically all of his works he sides with the older generation against the younger one—an unusual procedure for the comic genre—and in his autobiography, written in 1932, he describes his father and the years of his own childhood in such a way as to build up a contrastive image to the years to come, those in which he wrote.

As far as the child could see, society was a universe whose various segments, political, social, economic, and cultural, were in harmonious relationship to each other. The liberal rule of laissez faire governed personal interactions, and his parents were embodiments of this rule. They lived comfortably and, as far as they were concerned, their neighbors, the town, and the country were free to do the same: "In magnificent agreement my parents shared the triumphant knowledge: the bourgeois era in Germany around 1885 could not be compared . . . with any other period or any other age in any other part of the world. . . . God was not referred to often for the simple reason that in all circumstances one had, a priori, the greatest confidence in him" (*G*, vol. 10, pt. 1, p. 175).[2]

The same faith was to be put in His immediate representative on earth, the child's father. Not only had God created the best of all possible worlds, He had also made a law that every single thing on earth be kept in a state of utmost perfection, and He had set the father up as a guardian angel over this assembly of perfect objects: "At no time was he satisfied by that which was average; he wanted the utmost perfection in everything, as if God had appointed him as overseer, to assure that this His first commandment be unconditionally fulfilled on earth" (*G*, vol. 10, pt. 1, p. 174).

The implication of such a sentence becomes obvious in the

course of Sternheim's autobiography. The age of the son is dominated by industrialized and standardized mass production; the average has become the norm. Who, in the twentieth century, would still be able to imitate the gestures of the father who noticed the slightest deviation from perfection be it even in as simple a place as a delicatessen? "With the tips of his fingers he sampled the displayed dishes; I immediately saw in his eyes the flash of raptured agreement or the expression of a disappointment which crept into the very depths of his being" (*G*, vol. 10, pt. 1, p. 174).

To be sure, this perfectionist put some heavy demands on his surroundings. For prolonged periods of time the children had to sit quietly on a bench while he played the piano; after moving to Berlin, he sent weekly laundry baskets to distant Hanover because only there did washer women know how to starch his shirts properly. A missing comma in a school assignment could arouse his wrath—it was a flaw in God's established order.

If one adds up these and other details, the emerging picture could be that of a pedant or—worse even—of a petty tyrant compensating for his own weaknesses.[3] This, however, is not the intention which Sternheim pursues in remembering and relating such incidents. His father was, above all, a "character," an example of those unsplit personalities which later ages ceased to produce.

Sternheim experienced this contrast between the past and the present in both historical and geographical terms. Until 1884 his family lived in the provincial town of Hanover where his father owned a bank. His parents then moved to Berlin[4] to enjoy a life of comfortable semiretirement. Their various apartments were situated in good, although not the very best, living quarters of the city; for the summer, they owned a house near a provincial spa. Sternheim attended Berlin's most exclusive school and among his friends were the children of Fritz Simon, one of the leading bankers of the country. And yet the glorious times were over. As the autobiography puts it, a change affecting the political and economic spheres, the cultural values, and the mental and behavioral characteristics of his contemporaries took place about 1895.

The reasons for this change are easy to see. At the time,

Germany went through a period of hectic industrialization; she entered the era of modern capitalism at a speed unparalleled in any other country. Even for the upper echelons of the middle class, this development was traumatic. Incapable of competing with the new superrich, the members of this class saw themselves dangerously close to being reduced to the status of petty bourgeois and of being surrounded and outclassed by social parvenus who, according to the older standards, should have been far beneath them.

Sternheim's recollections of this process consist of a number of seemingly incongruous details, which, if added up, give a good impression of the trauma which parts of the bourgeoisie experienced in those years. Life suddenly became unattractively hectic; inventions like central heating and the light bulb, time-saving but impersonal devices, became ordinary household goods. The general topic of conversation centered around questions of finance. Names of industrialists and bankers replaced the cultural or political heroes of earlier decades. Human individuality ceased to be a major value and the feeling for individual greatness in politics or even for the individual's responsibility in economics faded away. Bismarck was replaced by puppets, and the patriarchally run and privately owned enterprises of the capitalistic founding fathers gave way to faceless and anonymous stockholding companies. Power structures thus lost their transparency. Uncultivated, vulgar people who had rightfully kept their mouths shut before suddenly emerged as opinion leaders, giving imprecise words to their vague feelings and indulging in sentimental verbiage.[5] The establishment of the department store turned people into obsessed consumers of cheap industrial products. Uniformity and total adaptation to social developments were postulated as the highest ideals of human behavior. Being "with it," being close to others, became the general ideal of existence.[6]

The trauma which is expressed in such observations haunted Sternheim throughout his life. It led to the central question of his work, which the author pursued with monomanic consistency: how can norms of aesthetic perfection and marks of personal distinction be retained under the conditions of mass production and the standardization of both men and goods?

This question is, of course, central to the works and lives of many of Sternheim's contemporaries,[7] and the attempts to answer it brought forth a wide spectrum of cultural products. At the one end of this spectrum, advocates of the *l'art pour l'art* doctrine concluded that aesthetic standards could be saved and used as a means of opposition only if the artist insisted on a clear separation of art from reality. At the other end, the official art and ideology of the period attempted to paint over the modern social and economic developments and the problems which they engendered. Wilhelminian Germany, in its own way, tried to save aesthetic norms by keeping up its identity as a non-Western, noncapitalistic country and by presenting itself through a multitude of architectural and representational facades. Office buildings, train stations, and factories had to conform with aesthetic concepts taken from a heroic past; there was, furthermore, the glamor world of the imperial court, of its army, its officers, and its generals, and there was, finally, the emperor, who presented himself as an embodiment of heroic leadership and as the model actor of his country.[8] A present-day historian has no difficulty in finding the effects of such compensatory stagecraft in practically all the cultural documents which the period produced. They are to be found in heroic paintings as well as in the poses in which the average citizen presented himself in his photographs. In other words, Wilhelminian society as a whole, as well as most of its middle-class members, developed its own version of aestheticism which is a far cry from the *l'art pour l'art* doctrine and yet grew out of very similar roots.

It can safely be said that Sternheim was not an advocate of the *l'art pour l'art* movement.[9] He always assumed that a determined individual could find ways and means to realize his aesthetic ideals within the realm of social reality; and Sternheim's own life can be read as an attempt to demonstrate such possibilities.[10] If the public sphere was adverse to ideals, then, according to Sternheim, private niches might provide the answer; if the middle classes were aesthetically repulsive, the aesthete could still put his hopes in the aristocracy or, conversely, in the proletariat.

Compared with the tenets of *l'art pour l'art*, Sternheim's version of aestheticism always remained on a low, if not trivial level. This had, however, one positive effect on his literary productivity. It permitted the author to remain within the limits of literary realism. On the other hand, Sternheim could never quite break out of what might be called the vicious circle of aesthetic opposition: the model figures which he presented to his public under the rubric of social protest always bear the essential characteristics of the typical bourgeois. Or, more generally speaking, Sternheim's aesthetic counterworlds are often an almost exact replica of the official taste of the times.[11]

The above portrait of Sternheim's father exemplifies well this more general observation. He is presented as an ideal figure; yet the poses in which he is shown are not very different from those which the average Wilhelminian bourgeois father struck. His most distinctive feature is his inner conviction and the lack of restraint with which he pursues that which was typical. It is precisely this lack of restraint which is characteristic of Sternheim's comic heroes and which gives them, according to the author, the status of model figures.

The following pages relate a number of episodes from young Sternheim's life which follow the same pattern. They show the adolescent in his flight from the mediocrity of middle-class existence, a flight which leads to nothing but an imitation of the feudal rites of the Wilhelminian empire.

The Pursuit of Aristocratic Glamor

If we can believe the autobiography, the child Sternheim saw in his father the first example of a quasi-heroic, or at least unsplit, personality. The adolescent found even more attractive models to turn to. Around the turn of the century, Berlin was not only one of Germany's industrial centers, it was also the stage on which the imperial court displayed its feudal relics. There was the glamorous world of young Prussian Junkers serving as *Garde* lieutenants in glorious regiments. Young Sternheim memorized their history to the last detail. He knew the pedigrees and the property of the European high aristocracy as listed in the handbook of the nobility, the *Gotha* almanac, as well as the pedigrees and achievements of famous racing horses. In his emulation of aristocratic rituals, he matched his father's pedantic perfectionism. As a university student in Munich he joined a distinguished upper-class fraternity, and not one of the middle-class Burschenschaften. His fragile body, however, rebelled against the rigorous drinking habits practiced in these circles. A second excursion into noble ranks ended on an equally disastrous note. Sternheim joined an aristocratic regiment in a provincial town near Berlin. Again, however, his health failed and he had to resign from active service before he could acquire the title of a reserve lieutenant.

For a present-day reader such incidents might appear as a new version of the comedy *Le Bourgeois Gentilhomme*. They are the comically inept attempts of a social climber to escape the conditions of his own milieu and to risk ridicule in the pursuit of goals which are not worth pursuing. Yet it is not in order to admit defeat that Sternheim relates these and similar incidents in his autobiography. He tells about them in a boasting and self-indulgent manner and tries to present himself less as a comic figure than as an admirable one. His excursions into noble ranks were an important goal: in his development toward manly maturity and in his acquisition of aristocratic manners. Never during his life, not even in periods where he openly sided with leftist anarchistic groups, did Sternheim conceal his admiration for the well-rounded personalities and the representational, quasi-theatrical life-style which the European aristocracy had, according to him, developed throughout the centuries.

Both Sternheim's social standing and his half Jewish origins made any genuine integration into aristocratic circles quite impossible. The only approximation of an aristocratic existence which was open to him was the life-style of a dandy, and it is not surprising that Sternheim was very much attracted by the possibilities which this style of existence offered. The stigma attached to a middle-class origin could be compensated for by the narcissistic cultivation of some eye-catching and fanciful idiosyncrasies. He who had been born into a social class which paid little attention to outward appearances could, as a dandy, try to turn his own person into a work of art and present himself to others as an actor on his own private stage. One of Sternheim's earliest poems announces this program in the following terms:

Original at any cost,
This be our device.
In being and acting
To be different from others.
To cultivate a sign
For others to recognize you.
To know how to do something
That one does not find elsewhere. . . .
This means: when you see
Something that pleases you
And that you consider distinguished
Don't imitate it.
On you it is no longer beautiful.
It is a copy.

(G, 9:24)

The poem not only gives clear expression to the characteristics and problems which have marked the history of European dandyism since its beginnings in the early nineteenth century, it also introduces another aspect of the vicious circle of aesthetic opposition. The dandy fights the standardizing tendencies of modern society by presenting himself as a unique and inimitable human being. In this respect, he emulates the aristocracy. He also knows, however, that he operates under incomparably worse conditions. The nobility, Sternheim later wrote in his comedy *The Snob.*, can be content with a correct uniformity of behavior since they already enjoy the advantage of birth. Their bourgeois imitator, on the other hand, has to excel by exhibiting his distinction. Worse even, he has to face the fact that his signs of distinction are imitable or even marketable. Today's originality is likely to be tomorrow's latest fad. The dandy thus finds himself in a continuous race. He has to flee the imitators who are at his heels and he has to be on his guard lest his own originality becomes the copy of someone else's.[12] He can reach security only if he can put his aristocratic allures on a somewhat more substantial basis, that is, if he can support his claim to distinction with sufficient financial means.

In 1902, Sternheim was introduced to this secure version of dandyism. He made the acquaintance of Ernst Schwabach, who was the co-owner of the most important German banking trust of the period and who invited him to his Silesian estate. Schwabach, the autobiographer Sternheim remarks, was the utmost in dandyism; he could have served as a model even for Oscar Wilde.

He was the first to show me how, even in a capitalistic era, a man with a great fortune could demonstrate good taste from beginning to end, from the interior furnishings to the livery of the servants, of the game keepers, who, in the evenings, lined up, with torches in their hands, on both sides of the day's kill which we, dressed for the evening, viewed from the front stairs. (*G*, vol. 10, pt.1, p. 224)

A few years later, Sternheim himself attained Schwabach's position. He married Thea Bauer, the rich heiress of an industrialist and he used some of his wife's money to build a palace outside of Munich complete with a monstrous gate, an ostentatious driveway, a library in the style of Louis XV, a picture gallery, and a small army of servants in olive green uniforms, a color chosen to blend in with the darker green of the park (*G*, vol. 10, pt. 1, p. 267). The dandy's dream of reaching the position of grand seigneur had come true; its realization, however, was still not free from comic side effects. The would-be aristocrat, one of Sternheim's friends facetiously remarked, was mainly reduced to playing the role of a tourist guide in his own palace.[13]

The Collector's Aesthetics

The lieutenant, the palace owner, the dandy: these were the social roles which Sternheim aspired to in his early years, that is, until approximately his thirtieth birthday. Writing literature, becoming an artist was not much more than a variation on the same theme. High social standing, a position of power, sexual success, and a dramatization of life: such qualities above all made an artist's life fascinating and attractive to the adolescent.

It is not surprising, therefore, that almost all of the many dramas which Sternheim wrote during his high school years share at least one common feature. Their typical hero is an artist who

closely resembles either an established aristocrat or a young lieutenant. If the hero is old, he is an artist of high repute, one of the
emperor's favorites;[14] if he is young, he leads a somewhat irregu-
lar, but highly respectable life in that he follows a strict code of
honor. He contracts gambling debts, discusses the necessity and
splendor of duels which he has to fight in order to save his sister's
reputation,[15] and he is dangerously attractive to women. His sexual power over others is a function of the quasi-divine position
which the artist can claim for himself. He is the creator of the
highest human values and can expect to be treated accordingly.
"Art is a goddess," "Honor art and her great prophets," we read in
one of the plays.[16] Can an artist, whose name happens to be Carl,
be loved? The thoughtful young girl has to answer ambiguously:
"Well yes, I love, I venerate him I should rather say, for he stands
too high above me."[17] Can a young married woman kiss an artist?
Yes she can. "You are allowed to kiss this man," she tells herself,
"since he cannot be measured on a human scale."[18]

Such examples can certainly be dismissed as the simple daydreams of an adolescent; yet they can also help to answer the question why Sternheim, the banker's son, embarked on a literary career in the first place. The plays which Sternheim wrote in the
five years after leaving school can hardly be considered more
promising. They mirror the efforts of a young author who thinks
that an imitation of the most conventional features of theater will
ensure him a stage success. In 1904 Sternheim met his future wife,
and it is certainly no coincidence that it was in the same year that
he wrote a neo-romantic play (*Ulrich and Brigitte*), which, in spite
of its epigonal character, does at least reach beyond the level of
mere banality. The husband of the rich and cultivated Thea Bauer
no longer had to run after an immediate stage success.[19] He and
his wife could, for a certain time, constitute their own public. "I
am reading *Ulrich and Brigitte* in bed," Sternheim writes in one of
his letters, "and I am deeply moved by my great art" (*G*, 7:798).
In another letter, he marvels at "how much we forgot the others
over Ulrich and Brigitte, how we were raised with them [i.e., with
the heroes of the play] into a world above the other one, and how
we succeeded in transferring their beauty into our lives" (*G*,
7:797).

Such sentences are in tune with the romanticizing elements of the play. In general, however, this pose as a romantic dreamer was only an episode. More typical and enduring is another and different concept of the artist which Sternheim espoused in these years, a concept which sees the artist in the role of a collector and arranger of valuable objects.

"Komm in den totgesagten Park und schau": this opening line of one of Stefan George's most famous poems also presents the gesture of a poet who sees himself as a collector. He has found something extraordinary and is willing to exhibit his finds, if not to the public, then at least to an intimate group of connoisseurs whom he can trust to be appreciative. Surrounded by intimates, the poet can almost refrain from using words; he can almost—and this would be his ideal—content himself with silently pointing at his treasures.

Sternheim has described the artist's work and his relationship to the public in much the same way. In a series of letters, written in 1905 and 1906, he describes the artist as if he were browsing through an antique shop looking for things of rare value. His eyes meet a variety of objects, but he is concerned only with those which exhibit some striking quality: "He removes an individual figure—any figure which is striking—from its place and regards it in respect to how it excels. He will then name this excelling particular quality which is to us a source of charm, of delight, or of annoyance" (*G*, 6:481).

The artist, Sternheim continues, is not the only one who approaches reality in this manner. The historian does so as well; he too is concerned with those individuals who represent some unique and exceptional quality. The historian, however, also has other goals in mind. He compares his finds, tries to trace their origin, or presents them to his readers as model figures. The artist, and he alone, can do justice to outstanding individuals. Art "is content simply to present them.—And thereby, it arouses pleasure. It never preaches . . . . it never prescribes anything (and it therefore does not cause embarrassment), but it speaks with sacred conviction: behold, I have found this" (*G*, 6:481).

The work of the artist cannot, according to this concept, be called truly productive. He does not create anything, but rather he has to develop an eye for the exceptional, for those rare jewels which have been produced by other forces, presumably by nature and history. Yet, there is a way in which the artist can at least supplement the productiveness of these forces. He can concentrate and arrange in one place that which in reality is scattered about. This, Sternheim says, is the function of drama. The playwright can, "within three hours, bring to life such a multitude of values as history hardly produces in millenia" (*G*, 6:479), values of a quality, furthermore, such as are never experienced by ordinary people in real life.

It is not difficult to recognize in such sentences the attitude of the palace owner. Both he and the playwright have to embark on a search for objects of some "excelling particular quality" with which to fill either the scenes of the stage or their as yet empty rooms. They are both collectors, although of different objects, and they both have to create an environment in which they can most effectively display their finds. It is not surprising in the light of such attitudes that Sternheim, in these years, developed a theory of drama which pays very little attention to the dramatic plot. The hero, Sternheim postulates, should not be a function of the action. On the contrary, all dramatic elements such as milieu, plot, scenes, ambience, and style, are to be evaluated only in regard to one question: do they serve to enhance the hero's valuable qualities? If they do not, they are out of place. Social tragedy, especially in its naturalistic form, is unacceptable since it presents the individual character as determined by general social conditions. The same is true for any drama revolving around an intrigue (*G*, 6:478). Sternheim demands that the dramatic action not be set in motion by any causes lying outside the hero's character or his sphere of command.

Such principles, it must be emphasized, do not refer only to theories of drama or effective staging. Taken together, they transcend the realm of art and amount to a *vision du monde*, to a particular and coherent mode of perceiving the world in general. Sternheim, one can safely add, adhered to this mode of perception throughout his life.

The collector Sternheim, as has already been said, confronts the world as if it were one giant antique shop. On its shelves, objects of greater or lesser quality are exhibited which can be examined and appreciated, bought or discarded. "Life," that is, nature and history, has produced these objects. The collector, however, is concerned with questions of origin only to the extent that they may have some impact on the object's rareness and thus its value. He is totally oblivious, furthermore, to the notion of *homo faber*, of man producing the means of his own existence. The historical chains of cause and effect and the concept of history as a continuous process are equally irrelevant. The *objet d'art* is thought to exist on a level above and beyond such processes. It is an autonomous, self-contained entity, and it should show traces neither of its original production nor of its original use. The same is still true if the *objet d'art* presents itself in a human form, that is, as a great personality. Great men are also objects of aesthetic contemplation and their value does not depend on how they affected their own society or the historical process. Nor does the aesthete have to be concerned with the historical conditions under which these great men lived. They are autonomous entities, and the outside world can, therefore, have no impact on their actions. "If we believe in a most profound truth in every man, that is, in every great man," Sternheim writes in one of his letters, "if he has recognized this most profound truth, how can 'the world' still affect him through its 'occurrences'?" (*G*, 6:478). The great man's position, finally, is an absolute one also in respect to ethical norms. Or rather, it is the collector's assumption that such norms are of a purely individualistic character and that they differ in content from one person to another. Sternheim can thus speak of morality, but he defines the moral person as one who will always follow in his actions that which he considers his very own duty, one which he does not share with anyone else. In ethics, "there can be no universal laws. In every individual case, each individual will come to conclusions about his duty which are totally his own" (*G*, 6:474).[20]

It is interesting to note that such concepts make it possible to discuss history and drama, society and art in the very same terms. Drama can be an exact replica of history because history is perceived with aesthetic categories. It constitutes an assembly of images whose major function is to give aesthetic pleasure to the knowledgeable and to serve as raw material for the artist. Contemporary society, finally, serves or rather ought to serve the very same function. Unfortunately, reality in twentieth-century society has become peculiarly deficient; as far as the collector can see, it is almost void of any unique values. Life is probably still productive but its rare products are no longer visible to the eye. They are hidden somewhere behind outer appearances and conventions; they are encaged in crusts and shells. It is at this point that the collector's mind begins to pursue a slightly different line of thought commonly designated by the term "vitalism."

Vitalist Perception

The assumption that "beauty" and "life" are mutually exclusive is one of the central tenets of turn-of-the-century aestheticism, and there is scarcely a great writer of the period who has not, at one time or another, presented himself as a martyr of his calling. The aesthete, the authors claimed, has to renounce the pleasures of life; literary creativity requires an ascetic existence, and only dilettantes can assume that art heightens the experience of life.[21]

Sternheim's life exemplifies quite well this ascetic trait of the modern writer. He apparently wrote down his works in long and physically exhausting sessions; he suffered a series of nervous breakdowns and when, after the war, he moved to a Swiss village, he reached an agreement with the mayor that no barking dogs and no cows were to be allowed within a certain distance of his house. Seen in this light, the walls around the park of Bellemaison and the artificial atmosphere of beauty within the park and the palace gain additional significance. If they give the owner an air of distinction, they also protect him from the outside world much in the same way as the fences around churchyards protect the dead from the noises of the living.

This, however, is not the interpretation which Sternheim himself gave to this secluded existence. On the contrary, he thought that only through seclusion does the individual have the chance to live his own life and to develop fully the vitalistic potential which is present in every person.[22] The forces of life, according to Sternheim, are deadened by the norms of social interaction. They can be reawakened by solitude; and the writer, in his self-chosen exile from society, does not negate the powers of life but rediscovers them for himself and recreates them for a world which is benumbed by daily routine.

The cult of life is a consistent element in Sternheim's works.[23] Within the comedies it often appears in scenes in which the comic heroes express their joy in ecstatically triumphant dances. There is no winner in these plays who is not, at the same time, healthier than his adversaries. In Sternheim's earlier writings, the same cult of life finds its expression in metaphors which equate the processes of artistic production and reception with phenomena belonging to the sphere of sexuality.

One of Sternheim's most interesting juvenile dramatic attempts concludes with a scene which features a sculptor who has finally regained his creative potency. The exclamations and gestures which accompany his work are clearly those of an orgiastic release.[24] In an essay on Van Gogh, Sternheim describes the Dutch painter as the first to "untie the belt" of his subject matter, Mediterranean nature, and the first to see it in its naked beauty. He also sees him "wallowing in its intestines" and then "raising to heaven" the "trophies" which he had found.[25] The artist Van Gogh is a rapist, at the very least. Michelangelo, to cite another example in which this metaphor is used, is a victim of rape. The culprit in this case is a force acting from within the artist. It was, Sternheim writes in a letter, "the overpowering force of his personality which raped the artist"[26] (*G*, 6:469). The reception of works of art can lead to similar experiences. While listening to Beethoven's *Fidelio*, Sternheim notes, he had the blissful feeling that he was "dissolving" and that his "inner being was floating out of its shell" (*G*, 6:477).[27] And finally he describes the women in several Renaissance paintings in the following terms: "Woman with her enormous vitality . . . sitting in front of us, dressed, in an attitude of the most perfect repose"; "Through her momentary weakness her whole power becomes gruesomely evident"; "The weak sweet sex and the crushing power of her loins; the colossally restrained power which waits

under every muscle of this body. . . . Oh God, this horrid calmness of power" (*G*, 6:468); "Every nerve quakes with passion" (*G*,
6:469).

Dilettantes in psychology should shy away from attempts at psy-
choanalytical explanations, and a look at the recurrent structural
patterns in the above quotations will, therefore, have to suffice.
They present the world as comprised of facades, of outer forms, of
surface appearances which bar the access to that which is essential.[28] The "trophies" which Van Gogh shows in his pictures were
hidden not only under a layer of clothing, but also under the skin
of the body, a second layer which the artist must pierce to reach
that which is valuable in his object. This distinction between the
outside and the inside also characterizes the artist's own psyche. He
too consists of an outer crust, an enveloping shell, and some liquid
mass or fiery nucleus which longs for an outlet. To dissolve, to flow
out of the shell, to ejaculate, to become fluid constitutes one of the
most blissful feelings which can be experienced. And yet, the shell
is not only a wall which bars access and imprisons, it is also a guar-
antee of order and safety. The forces hidden behind the surfaces are
sinister, dangerous, and chaotic. When they erupt, they are likely
to be destructive.

This ambivalence is most clearly expressed in Sternheim's descriptions of Renaissance paintings. The outside facade of quiet serenity which the portrayed women present to the contemplative
eye is attractive in itself. Yet even more attractive and fascinating
is that which lurks behind this surface: the awesome power of life
as it appears in sexuality. Sternheim views these paintings as a
mouse might watch a snake which is about to devour it; and it understandable that he concludes with a praise of neo-classicism. Art
is assigned the task of unveiling the overpowering forces of life; in
doing so, however, it must also contain them. Painters are, accordingly, evaluated as to their success in reconciling movement
with calmness, the pathos of emotion with the serenity of pure
forms.

Apollo's harp, Nietzsche had written thirty years earlier, is no
match for Bacchus's flutes; the pure forms of art cannot withstand
for long the assault of the bacchanals.[29] This observation applies to

Sternheim as well. In his early letters he sides with Apollo against Dionysus, with Raphael against Michelangelo, and he explicitly concludes that it is the artist's function to contain chaos. The basic experiences, however, which are described in the above quotations seem to contradict such a conclusion. The sight of powers contained may have provided Sternheim with a feeling of security; yet, it is the act of breaking through or of breaking out which obviously arouses a feeling of joy and happiness.

It is not surprising, therefore, that Sternheim, in the course of his literary development, switches from the side of order to that of anarchy, and that he does so not only in aesthetics. The metaphoric system sketched above has to be interpreted within the general dialectics of suppression and freedom, of anarchy and order; it could easily be transferred from the sphere of sexuality and aesthetics to the realm of social and political theory. The novellas which Sternheim wrote during the war years use similar metaphors to describe practically all aspects of human life. Those who follow the norms of society, Sternheim tries to demonstrate, form "crusts" and are cut off from the sources of life; they can solve their existential crises only by regaining access to the fiery nuclei hidden both within themselves and underneath the surfaces of the surrounding world. During the revolutionary years of 1917 to 1920, Sternheim uses the same imagery to propagate his version of a cultural revolution. Breaking through crusts now means to break through the ideologies produced by bourgeois society and to make accessible to man the inexhaustible aesthetic and vitalistic energies of life.

Conformism and Literary Productivity

The emulation of social glamor, dandyism, the cult of life, and of the "great personality," the quest for "striking" values, the collector's attitude toward history and society—such characteristics do not, at first sight, seem to provide a twentieth-century author with a fertile ground for literary productivity. It is, therefore, understandable that a number of critics have dismissed many of the above traits as the author's personal affair and as irrelevant for an understanding of his work.[30] Others have come to the opposite conclusion. They have dismissed Sternheim's works with the argument that they are not much more than an expression of "Wilhelminian neuroticism."[31] Neither of these two approaches and conclusions, however, seems justified. Literary works are man-made products and cannot, therefore, be evaluated without a knowledge of their producers and of the social conditions under which their authors were formed and to which they responded. The knowledge of such conditions, motivations, and intentions, on the other hand, does not provide the critic with sufficient grounds for a final verdict. As one critic aptly remarked, the demonstration of an author's neuroses, idiosyncrasies, and weaknesses should not be used as an argument against his work, but rather as a stimulus for the question: how did he succeed in making them literarily productive.[32] For Sternheim's work this is, indeed, one of the key questions, and the material presented so far may already allow a few tentative answers.

Hans Mayer once noted that some of the qualities of Thomas Mann's novels originate from the author's ability to turn himself into a camera and to store in his memory the peculiarities of his acquaintances for a possible use in one of his stories. The same observation applies to Flaubert and to such "dandies" as Baudelaire and Oscar Wilde—all of whom Sternheim admired—and it applies to Sternheim's work as well. Among twentieth-century German playwrights, Sternheim excels through his ability to notice, and to represent on the stage, the most minute details of the poses and mannerisms with which his contemporaries enacted their social roles. This acuity of perception can hardly be understood without references to Sternheim's own pursuit of social glamor. His social poses have at least one common feature: in various ways they turn the person into an expert spectator; they are an excellent school for man's observational faculties. The collector must, by necessity, focus his attention on those "nuances"[33] which set his finds apart from that which is average; for the dandy again only the nuances count and, in the same way, the social climber has to develop an eye for those almost inperceptible mannerisms which cultural elites develop as a shield against unwanted intruders. As a way of life, dandyism is certainly not without its comic features; as a preparatory school for a writer of comedies it is not to be despised.

Sternheim's position as a palace owner was equally ambivalent. As his own tourist guide, he played a comic role. Yet, there was, as Sternheim later observed in his autobiography, also a possibility of putting his palace to a productive use. It could be a gathering place for the celebrities of his time, and the host could play the part of a stage or film director who screens potential actors for his next production. The required qualification was, as can be expected, some display of originality: "Of the several hundred celebrities from all fields who had been our guests scarcely half a dozen had been capable of enriching us, be it only to the extent that we could perceive them as particular entities.[34] The rest enacted their own silence; they were the bad copies of already flawed models" (*G*, vol. 10, pt. 1, p. 270).

Once more, these sentences give expression to the frustrations of the collector who, in his search for originals, is confronted only with bad copies. Half a dozen personalities among several hundred celebrities! These few at least could be used as the raw material of literature.[35] For this is how Sternheim, in his autobiography, understood his own literary procedure and his literary "calling": "to give, through condensing, real life to the vaguely lived existences" of his contemporaries (*G*, vol. 10, pt. 1, p. 268).

Sternheim, such may be a first conclusion to be reached by such observations, was capable of conforming to the laws of theater and of fully exploiting its potentials because he perceived himself and those around him in terms of the stage. This mode of perception, it is true, ignores many aspects of social reality, chief among them the laws of the market which, in a capitalistic society, determine not only the principles of production but also, to a great extent, the relations between human beings. It is the overwhelming influence of this determinant and the ensuing "abstractness" of human existence which has led other twentieth-century playwrights to a search for new modes of dramatic presentation. Sternheim's work is almost free of such innovative attempts. His plays consequently fail as soon as they tackle questions belonging to the realms of society, history, and economics at large. They are at their best as long as the playwright restricts his presentation to those facets of modern life which can be grasped in direct visual terms: the gestures, the masks, and the poses which men use in order to express themselves or to impress each other.

For both the collector and the playwright, paradise would be a society consisting of "striking personalities," of men who, without any sign of inhibition, display their characters and enact their self-chosen roles. Sternheim's vitalistic tenets point in the same direction. They postulate that man's freedom depends on his ability to break through the layers of social convention, to disregard the norms of common morality, and to give free expression to his innermost instincts and drives. In other words, both the aesthete and the vitalist abhor the appearance of compromise, of moderation, of lukewarm actions; if necessary, they prefer the ruthless man to one who is inhibited by doubts and moral qualms. Sternheim's statement that he intended "to give . . . real life to the vaguely lived existences" of his contemporaries thus has a two-fold meaning. "Real life" is the prerequisite for a dramatic character; it is also, for Sternheim, the primary condition of human freedom, and its presentation on the stage is meant to increase the liveliness of society and its individual members.[36]

The history of Sternheim criticism shows that the success of his plays does not depend on this emancipatory program. While admiring the realism and the theatrical effectiveness of Sternheim's works, most critics have chosen to ignore the author's vitalistic and aestheticist tenets. His comic heroes have thus not been appreciated as models of human freedom but rather have been regarded as satirical denunciations of a bourgeoisie which was in the process of shedding all ethical and social norms. The discussion of Sternheim's works in the following chapters will, at least indirectly, give ample support to such interpretations. It will, at the same time, try to trace the inner logic of his plays and the development of his thinking. Sternheim, it will be seen, attempted to demonstrate that a clear line of distinction can be drawn between a free, self-oriented, and aesthetically attractive expression of individual drives on the one hand and their functionalization on behalf of society on the other. These demonstrations are not always convincing. In pursuing his arguments, however, Sternheim developed an uncommonly keen eye both for the psychological mechanisms which governed the interactions of his contemporaries and for the various ways in which his—and not only his—society used its cultural offerings, norms, and idols to divert its members from pursuing their immediate personal interests.

Don Juan, the drama which will be discussed in the following chapter, was written between 1905 and 1909. It still falls within Sternheim's early period and can be classified as the author's last and most ambitious attempt at the tragic genre. Stylistically it bears all the features which have so far been characterized and downgraded as "Wilhelminian." And yet *Don Juan* cannot easily be passed over in silence. It is the first work with which Sternheim succeeded in attracting public attention;[37] the play is remarkable, and in many passages fascinating, as a blatant expression of the aesthetic, vitalistic, and sexual daydreams of the period, and further it contains many of the themes which characterize Sternheim's later writings. A discussion of the play thus also helps to demonstrate the basic unity of his oeuvre.

Chapter Two

Don Juan

The scene is in front of the cathedral of Valladolid. Masses of people either sit on benches or, held back by police, walk around the square and the passway on the left side of the stage. From the grand stairway the laughter of young noblemen is to be heard. Preceded by gentlewomen and gentlemen, the spring festival procession approaches to the chimes of the church bell. There are the acolytes, the clergy, the bishop, and rows of young girls clad in white, with roses in their hair. The festivity starts with the bishop's recitation and the girls' choral responses. From within the church, an organ can be heard accompanying a second choir assembled there.

This short description of the opening scene of *Don Juan* gives a first impression of the aesthetic intentions which Sternheim pursued in this tragedy. He overwhelms his spectator with a multitude of brilliant colors, harmonious sound effects, and all the other aesthetic glamor which may be considered part of a *Gesamtkunstwerk*. It is certainly this genre which Sternheim had in mind,[1] and he followed its principles throughout the play. He stages grandiose battles and depicts picturesque army camps, the graceful atmosphere of a ball room and the somber dignity of the Escorial, the interior of a Gothic cathedral and the gaiety of a bucolic pasture where young shepherdesses go skinny dipping and are almost raped by the hero. *Don Juan* was to be, in the author's own words, "more beautiful than a human mind can imagine" (*G*, 7:812).

More beautiful and—one might add—more significant. The play's central character is, of course, the legendary Don Juan Tenorio, the archetype of the insatiable lover. In Sternheim's version, however, he also bears the traits of Don Juan d'Austria, the famous sixteenth-century general, bastard son of the Emperor Charles V and victorious general of the Spanish-Turkish Battle of

Lepanto. This blending of two figures into one allowed Sternheim, first of all, to combine love and sexuality with politics and heroic warfare. Even more, it allowed him to ascribe to his hero a multitude of sublime meanings. According to the author, his Don Juan was to be as glorious a general as Napoleon; he was to be, however, a Napoleon with a "heart" (*G*, 7:836); he was to be the model after which Cervantes fashioned his *Don Quixote*;[2] he was to be the opposite of Philipp II, the first representative of modern *Realpolitik*; and, above all, he was to be a predecessor to Goethe's Faust and, at the same time, a modern super-Faust. The division of the tragedy into two parts, as well as a number of specific scenes, is clearly fashioned after Goethe's model, and so is one of the mottos of the play: "I love him who covets the impossible."

The history of the arts in the nineteenth century shows clearly that the imagination becomes peculiarly unproductive if allowed to roam about freely in an unrestricted and unprincipled quest for beauty.[3] Sternheim's play is no exception to this rule. In his attempt to create an epitome of beauty, the author ended up compiling and copying the beauty of past ages. In many respects, therefore, Don Juan can be considered the literary equivalent of the architectural monstrosities which are so characteristic of the Wilhelminian era. And yet the discussion of the play cannot stop at this point. The official art of the period was produced to serve representational and politically affirmative functions. It was to help in stabilizing society and in supporting the empire's imperialistic political goals. There is no question, however, that Sternheim used the same aesthetic means for oppositional and quasi-anarchistic intentions. This leads, within the play, to a number of paradoxes which keep reoccurring on various levels and which characterize not only the aesthetic dimensions of the play, but also the treatment of various psychological and political themes. The would-be anarchist, it turns out time and again, cannot escape the very social mechanisms which he fights: the hero, in giving expression to his most individual desires, ends up by expressing the most common wishes of his contemporaries. It is, above all, because of this paradoxical relationship between subjective intentions and objective results that the play still elicits some interest today.

Expressing desires: This, of course, is the major function of Don Juan's sexual pursuits. Sternheim's hero is as ardent a lover as any of his literary predecessors; he surpasses them, however, in the degree of ferocity with which he pursues women and by the number of atrocities which he commits in such pursuits. In presenting this line of dramatic action, the author succeeds in amassing a veritable pandemonium of pubertarian daydreams. In the name of love, Don Juan furiously persecutes a girl and her mother; he kills a father, plans rape and poisoning, sets a house afire, or desperately tries to find substitutes for his love in the form of a whore or a dummy figure. All these actions are noteworthy, above all, for Sternheim's surprising degree of frankness and for his disregard of social taboos.

The second part of the tragedy raises these pubertarian drives onto a somewhat more sublimated level. Don Juan's love Maria has died, and the hero learns to draw satisfaction from sexual fantasies, rather than from sexual acts. Here again, Sternheim blends several themes into one. In Don Juan's imagination, Maria becomes undistinguishable from the Holy Virgin. The lover, consequently, dreams of a mystical union with his love. Yet, this seeming spiritualization allows Sternheim an even more open portrayal of sexual drives. There is nothing sweeter for this hero than to imagine himself licking Maria's boots and being crushed under her heels; there is nothing he wishes more ardently than to return to his mother's womb. Don Juan curses his mother "who untied me from her lap and forced me / to go out into a barren world" (*G*, 7:664); and he expresses the vision of the mystical union, of becoming one and the same with the "undivided essence of Jesus Christ" in the following terms:

> Your Body is everything.
> Blood sprang over to me from your arteries and skin,
> from your body I receive the sap and clay.
> Your flesh swells and forms red clouds
> around my forehead, my senses feel
> a warm cave in a round shape, I am slipping
> and mount and mount and vanish whirling.
>
> (*G*, 7:665)

The Oedipal wish, which is combined here with masochistic desires and with images borrowed from Catholic mysticism, reappears toward the end of the play on the level of rational discussion. Oedipus is presented as a model figure. Like other heroes of Greek mythology, he lived, according to Don Juan, in an era where man's "wild longing" did not hit upon the "walls" of social morality. Oedipus could thus realize his wish of "holding, for one starlit night, his mother in his arms like a sweet woman and of forgetting himself with her" (*G*, 7:689); It was up to later ages, Don Juan continues, above all, to judge human activities and desires from the point of view of social utility.

This reinterpretation of the Greek myth is an especially illuminating example of the above-mentioned dialectics both of anarchy and order and of the most individual turning into the most common. Against the categories of social morality and utility, Don Juan holds up his belief that man is "only blissful in himself" (*G*, 7;689) and that the only valuable social contacts are based on the principle of mutual aesthetic appreciation. The hero is interested in his fellow human beings only for those features which are "deliciously unique and incalculable" (*G*, 7:690).[4] It is, once more, the collector who speaks here. His utopian ideal would be a society where general norms and rational constraints have been suspended and where man is free to follow his very own and incomparable desires, beliefs, and longings. For Don Juan, Oedipus is such an ideal figure. He is both a rebel and an individualist. Yet, Oedipus has also, and very convincingly, been described as a figure who, far from pursuing any incomparable desires, expresses one of the most universal features of man's psyche. Sternheim's concept of individualism thus coincides with that which some psychologists consider archetypal, and his attempt to present Oedipus as a model of heroic freedom is equally ambiguous. Post-Freudian psychology has sufficiently demonstrated that the Oedipal wish originates from the structures of patriarchal societies. Within this structure Oedipus is a rebel. And yet, even when he slays his father and fulfills his erotic desires, he is still the product and the prisoner of the very society which he fights. Sternheim's hope that the free expression of subconscious wishes would set man free quite simply ignores the fact that such wishes, more than anything else, have been produced and formed under the influence of historical conditions.[5]

Sternheim does not ignore, it has to be added, a very similar dialectic which is characteristic of the relationship between the aesthetic ideal of heroism on the one hand and modern political and social systems on the other. Like many heroes of German classical drama, Sternheim's Don Juan derives part of his aesthetic dignity from the fact that he is a late representative of medieval heroism;[6] and it is, above all, the tragedy of his life that he is born too late and that he cannot withstand the historical changes set in motion by the emergence of the territorial state.

There had been a time, the audience is told in the opening of the play, when each person was his own sovereign; now, however, under the reign of Philipp II, the majesty of the individual is concentrated in one person, the monarch: "A complete image of Spain's majesty, an image which once everyone presented, only the king presents it now. He has sucked into his only person the proud self-confidence of the people and the pride of over a thousand Spanish grandes" (G, 7:499). These sentences refer to the development of the modern state; they do so, however, less in political than in aesthetic terms, The king presents an "image of Majesty," and it is "pride" not power which his subjects have lost. Seen under this aspect, the survival of heroism is still possible. Although Don Juan is incapable of regaining his power, he can still retain his pride.

Don Juan cannot, however, openly present his proud character to the people. In modern societies—and here Sternheim reflects upon the psychological effects of the new power structures—the hero is no longer seen as a symbol of the autonomy of all men. In confronting him, the people desire not to be his equal, to emulate his qualities and thus to regain their liberty, but rather they regard him as a political leader and wish to become his followers. The subjects of Philipp II—to return to the level of the play—indulge in dangerous fantasies. They are dissatisfied with the moderate conservativism of their monarch and dream not of a restitution of their autonomy, but of great historical movements and of great heroes who will lead them toward new goals: "And the whole nation expects, as it hardly ever did before, the hero's surprising action. It offers its arm to him for a thorough bloodletting and an enormous loss of its sap. The nation wants to bleed, it wants to be purged for the new century" (*G*, 7:686).

One can safely transfer such sentences to the political realities of Sternheim's own time: the German people have grown tired of the conservativism of the Bismarck era; they dream of political fireworks, of the power displays of imperialism, if not of worse incarnations of political leadership. They will actively support political actions or political movements which degrade them to the state of lifeless ogres.

In this situation an heroic existence and its presentation in tragedy results in a blatant paradox. On the one hand, the hero is functionalized as a leader as soon as he shows himself publicly; and, although unwillingly, he thus contributes to the historical process of power concentration. On the other hand, he is, almost by definition, a public figure and can claim his title only if his heroism is perceptible at least in some fashion.

In an obvious attempt to solve this problem Sternheim alludes, at one point, to Don Quixote, whom he interprets as a medieval knight who consciously presents himself in the mask of a fool. Nobody, except a few insiders, will recognize the hero in this guise of folly; and, above all, society cannot put to any use the senseless heroic acts which he commits. Sternheim's hero Don Juan uses a similar cloak. In one scene which Sternheim considered particularly important, Don Juan climbs over a high fence although an open gate is only a few feet away. In a boyish act of definition he shuns the easy way and refuses to comply with the economy of means and goals.[7] He further refuses to yield to reality. His love has died, yet she is with him in his imagination and she sits in an empty coach which follows the hero wherever he goes.

To prevent any social abuse of his own acts, the hero has to put on the mask of the fool or—at best—of the romantic dreamer. Under this guise he is unrecognizable and useless. This solution may work for the lover: both the Oedipal and the mystic form of eroticism are socially dysfunctional.[8] It is hard to see, however, how the same solution can be applied to the general. As the leader of the Spanish army, as the victorious admiral of the Battle of Lepanto, Don Juan performs political functions in the service of the monarch. As if he wanted to anticipate this objection, Sternheim has his hero declare that he does not fight wars for any political purpose. If he is a hero, he acts solely for the glory of Maria. Or—to put the same thought in more concretely political terms—he abhors a concept of warfare which serves the expansionist policies of modern nations. He follows, instead the model of the Greek heroes in their war against Troy—or, at least, his own version of this war:

> There the nation died
> which for the sake of one woman
> faced, with sacred conviction, the horrors
> of furious wars,
> which sacrificed its best men because its mind
> would not accept the fact: Helen the Greek
> among barbarians.
>
> (G, 7:688)

Once again, these sentences demonstrate Sternheim's awareness of the political developments of his time, as well as the futility of his attempt to use images of heroism as a means of political opposition. Modern wars are indeed mostly fought for imperialistic goals. This fact, however, has not excluded the abundant and very effective use of heroic images in political propaganda. On the contrary, the more difficult it was to legitimize a war in terms of the individual's own interests, the more it was necessary for political leaders to take refuge in the stimulation of aesthetic fantasies. Thus, disregarding the historical particulars, Don Juan's ideal image of war reads almost like an anticipation of the German propaganda of 1914 and 1939.

The genre of heroic tragedy—this is the result of all the above observations—allowed no escape from the vicious circle of aesthetic opposition. If it could be used at all, then only for official political propaganda. In the course of World War I, Sternheim became aware of this fact himself[9] and he later attacked tragedy in general as a highly ideological genre.[10] The insight both into the psychological tendencies of modern man to abdicate his autonomy and into the social uses of aesthetic fantasies, furthermore, remained one of the central themes of Sternheim's works. This insight leads, on the level of comedy, to a glorification of middle-class "heroes" who, by refusing to open their minds to the allurements which society offers, succeed in safeguarding their freedom. As an author of comedies, Sternheim by no means gave up the vitalistic and aesthetic tenets which he pursued in *Don Juan*. By transferring them to a different genre, he did, however, change their character, and he could, to a certain extent, avoid the inner contradictions which are characteristic of his early works.

Chapter Three
The Bloomers

Exit the tragic hero with his royal festivities, his murders, incendiaries, historical battles, and grandiose opera scenes; enter the petty bourgeois.[1] His name is, in the first of the comedies, Theobald Maske; he is a clerk, lives in a modest three-bedroom apartment with the facilities midstairs. He tends to have outbreaks of rage and apparently beats his wife for minor transgressions. He can be placated, however, with the prospect of an extra delicious roast of lamb. He is in favor of law and order and makes sure that his wife does not forget what her "world" is, namely, the kitchen and the dust-covered floor. On the other hand, he is not disinclined to enjoy an extra beer or a mistress if such commodities can be obtained in moderation and without undue risks to his health and his reputation, two assets which he treasures indeed. Most of all, however, he likes his own four walls and the limited dimensions of his familiar world. He knows very well how people can be endangered by their fantasies, especially people like himself who live on limited incomes and do not yet enjoy the freedom which only retirement benefits can bestow.

Summaries of literary works or descriptions of literary figures can hardly be objective. Where they pretend to describe, they already perceive and render their object in the light of some thesis. In this case, the thesis might be that Sternheim's play is a satire on the middle classes and that its central figure represents what, from romanticism to the twentieth century, was contemptuously called a philistine existence.[2] With his limited intellectual curiosity, his sole interest in petty comfort, his ostentatious nonunderstanding of man's higher aspirations, the philistine Maske has seemed to most critics to be an object of bewilderment, satirical derision, and disgust. He has appeared not as a human being but as his caricature.

For Sternheim's contemporaries, there were further reasons to support such an interpretation. They noted the uninvolved, cold, and seemingly mocking presentation of the figures, they observed the shocking lack of interpersonal dialogues and of human understanding, and they could further base their reading of the play on their knowledge of the author's character. Sternheim's critics knew about his palace and his dandyistic attitudes; they observed his appearances in public, his self-presentation in front of the curtain, where he seemed to enjoy hisses more than applause and impressed onlookers by the haughty, blasé mockery with which he could look down at an enraged audience.[3] In his first more widely circulated publication, an essay on Van Gogh which had appeared in Franz Blei's journal *Hyperion*, Sternheim had denounced the German public for being unworthy of being spoken to by the likes of a Carl Sternheim;[4] and according to the recollections of Siegfried Jacobsohn—once a schoolmate of Sternheim's and then a leading theater critic—he had displayed such characteristics already in the days of his youth. Sternheim's plays—this was Jacobsohn's evaluation—were excellent comedies presenting life as it would be observed from the "mockers' bench."[5]

The author himself suggested a very different reading of his plays. In 1918, toward the end of World War I, he published a short article, "Saving the Middle Classes," which was meant as a preface to a second edition of his comedies (*G*, 6; 45–47). Bourgeois reality, he says there, is to be found in the sphere of economic pursuits and financial transactions, spheres unknown to the general public. Writers, instead of shedding light on these spheres, have only shown stylized dreamworlds, or they have, in the naturalistic vein, concentrated on marginal segments of society. The leading circles of the bourgeoisie have thus been able to erect a beautiful facade, "gas clouds of sentiments, and trenches of metaphors," behind which they could go about their business without public interference. "Saving the middle classes," then, means doing away with literary conventions, showing bourgeois reality as it is and presenting a model hero who has freed himself from the cultural illusions which still enslave his audience. This is exactly what Sternheim's comedies, according to the preface, are all about. They demonstrate the incongruity between the "cherished ideals of the middle classes" and the real but suppressed psychic drives of their individual members. Furthermore, they show a hero free of such inner contradictions. "To be sure he does not excel in picture-book virtues which poets, up to the present, have sung about, but in contrast to his rotten philistine surrounding, he is aware of his own resources and fanatically obsessed by his own goals" (*G*, 6:46). Far from pursuing any ironic or satiric intentions, Sternheim goes on, it had been his goal to present his audience with a model character and with a positive message: "If man wants to use his inner vital energy, he must not listen to traditional roundelays, but to his fresh individual sound, regardless of the names which middle class mentality might give to his sometimes brutal tinge of character" (*G*, 6:47).

A philistine existence as a cure for the ailments of the middle classes, brutality as a praise-worthy trait of behavior, successful satire as a presentation of model characters: it seems understandable that Sternheim's publisher was reluctant to print this preface. Apparent absurdities do not promote the sale of books. For the present purposes, however, it seems advisable to discuss Sternheim's plays first of all in terms of the author's intentions before any other lines of interpretation are pursued.

The Real World of the Middle Classes

Making the most of things: this is the goal which entirely determines Maske's actions. It may be a petty goal, yet it is one which has been very effective in the ascent of the bourgeois and, like any good bourgeois and like any good comedy figure, Maske is methodical and unrelenting in its pursuit. He can only dispose of very limited means, both financially and intellectually, and therefore must be careful not to squander and not to be led into temptation. His assets as well as his security lie within his own four walls and in an appearance of utter mediocrity and normality. Only in this disguise and within this limited realm can he live according to his desires and exploit his share of enjoyments to their fullest degree. "My freedom is lost," he says, "if the world pays any special attention to me. My insignificance is the cloak of invisibility under

whose cover I can follow my penchants and my innermost nature"
(R, 121; G, 1:96).[6] Others, he adds, may act differently if they
wish. As long as they do not, with their strivings, intrude into his
little niche, they are of no concern to him. Maske cannot, of
course, afford to apply this liberal attitude to his own wife, Luise.
She is pretty and may attract attention. She likes the trappings of
fashion which make harmless breasts protrude (R, 82; G, 1:30),
and which turn ordinary women into irresistible beauties. Luise is
not allowed any of this. And yet her husband seems to be fighting
a losing battle. The couple—this is the event preceding the play's
action—has been out in order to watch a royal parade. Luise, while
stretching to have a better look at the king's coachman, has lost
her bloomers. The little accident may have—and indeed has—attracted the attention of others, and Maske can already foresee the
catastrophes which will put an end to his benign existence.

Society presents itself to Maske under two major aspects. For the
office clerk it is a dependable source of money and will later provide him with retirement benefits. On the other hand, it is a force
intent upon depriving him of his autonomy. The social world
consists of a set of rules and expectations; it requires compliance
and punishes deviations. It is to be feared even more, however, for
its allurements. It seduces its members to turn into unrestrained
consumers; it does all it can to arouse their imagination and to excite their dreams. Why did Luise lose her pants if not for love of
fantasy? Girls, and girls only, Maske sermonizes, have a right to
dream because they have no access to reality. Married women, on
the other hand, are surrounded with real things up to their ears.

THEOBALD: Where is the real world? (He grabs her head and strikes it
against the table.) Down here in the saucepan, on your dust-coated living
room floor and not up there in the sky, do you hear? Is this chair polished? No, filth! Has this cup a handle? Wherever I lay my hands, the
world is splitting apart. Crack after crack in an existence like yours. Hor-
rible! (R, 80; G, 1:29)

There is perhaps only one such crack in Maske's own existence:
his newspaper. He reads one every day, but he does so with cau-
tion. After all, what are newspapers for if not to flood the imagi-

nation and to invite ordinary people to marvel at the wonders of
the world which are quite beyond their reach. Twice during the
play he reads about a certain sea serpent which has supposedly been
sighted in the South Pacific. What, he asks, is the possible use of
such a report? "Doesn't it at the most excite my imagination?" (*R*,
83; *G*, 1:33). Maske will have done of it. To him the mere "news
of such odd things is repulsive. Literally repulsive" (*R*, 144; *G*,
1:134).

Herbert Marcuse has spoken of the terror of the modern consumer society. Sternheim would have agreed with him and so
would Maske had he been able to understand the word, which is
doubtful. For Maske, the general expectation that people ought to
acquire knowledge or do something for their minds is one of the
most formidable social instruments to divert them from their real
pleasures. Maske is confronted with such expectations in the course
of act 3 by his two antagonists, the poet Scarron and the hairdresser Mandelstam. Both have witnessed Luise's little accident
and have immediately rented a room in Maske's apartment in order
to be closer to their heroine. Although they should be natural opponents, they unite in the third act in their bewilderment at
Maske's conspicuous lack of cultural ambition and in their efforts
to educate him. The living room, which should be the antecham-
ber to Luise's bedroom, is thus transformed into a salon, and the
two lovers play the part of proponents of various metaphysical positions. They speak of progress and technical inventions, drop the
names of Schwarz, Luther, Goethe, and Wagner and advocate such
Nietzschean and Darwinian tenets as the survival of the fittest, the
denunciation of pity, the glory of strength, and the metaphysical
inferiority of the female. Theobald, who is unversed and uninter-
ested in theoretical abstractions, translates everything said against
him into concrete terms, which, of course, effects a complete reversal of meaning.

The possession of such a lovely young woman, he is told, should
motivate him to improve himself and to do something for his education. Theobald does not quite follow. After all, his wife is only a
tailor's daughter. But then, he will try:

THEOBALD: We could go to the zoo tomorrow. They have got themselves a giraffe.
MANDELSTAM (Laughing): giraffe!
THEOBALD: What is there to laugh at about that?
MANDELSTAM: I think my thoughts.
THEOBALD: If I'm to be honest, left to myself, I'd never have hit on the idea of looking at such an animal. I am really averse to such flamboyancies and eccentricities of nature. But since Herr Scarron is pressing me so hard, I want to do something to educate myself. (*R*, 120; *G*, 1:95)

In another, similar scene, the topic of conversation is Nietzsche's hymn to power. "Nietzsche," Scarron explains, "teaches the gospel of our times. The individual blessed with energies will give direction to the boundless masses of men and set their minds on a goal.[7] Might is the peak of happiness." Answers Theobald: "Might is delight, I agree. I knew that while I was still at school when I made others suffer at my hands" (*R*, 115; *G*, 1:87).

The principle which Sternheim follows in such conversations, as he does throughout the play, is not uncommon for the language of comedy. In seeming agreement with his opponents and with irrefutable logic, Theobald reduces ideas and cultural values to their lowest possible meaning. Nietzsche's glorification of strength is a triviality for someone who used to bully his schoolmates; education is to be obtained through a visit to the zoo, its goal is to make one familiar with nature's oddities.

Yet, it is not only a comic, but also a bourgeois principle which structures such statements.[8] Maske looks at the outside world with the eye of an investor who is confronted with a business proposition. There are three main questions to be asked: Can he afford the price? What is the ratio of expense and return? Is the proposition secure? Other concerns may be interesting; they are, however, irrelevant. It is unimportant, for instance, to speculate about the truth or falsehood of some abstract philosophical tenet. All that counts is its usefulness in daily life. Maske is quite willing to admit to Scarron that there may be a "transcendental difference" between male and female. However, "speaking from my personal experience, I can't convince myself that it would have brought me advantages in my marriage if I had strengthened and expressed this feeling of difference" (*R*, 119; *G*, 1:93). Such pragmatic skepticism seems appropriate to Maske vis-à-vis any of the so-called cultural values. At best, the pursuit of such values is comparable to the acquisition of long-term bonds which may mature only after the buyer's death.

THEOBALD: My life span is seventy years. With the mental attitude I have acquired, I can enjoy quite a lot of things in my own way in that time. If I wanted to embrace a more exalted way of looking at things, that is, your rules, with my limited talents, I'd scarcely learn in a hundred years what to do. (*R*, 117; *G*, 1:90)

The investor's view toward profitability also dictates Maske's relationship to his fellow human beings. Here again, he will strictly abstain from squandering his energies and from giving free rein to his imagination. His wife is, above all, to be considered in her qualities of housekeeper and cook. As a sexual object, she is a potential danger. The picture over the couple's bed shows "The Lion fighting Boa Constrictor." Conjugal sex produces children who are expensive to raise and might upset Maske's balanced budget. The hero has, therefore, touched his wife only once during the first year of marriage and then only by accident. Illicit sex is another matter. A friend of Luise's, a Fräulein Deuter, comes in handy for this purpose. Here too, however, economizing is a must. Deuter's love declarations—"Do you love me? . . . From now on every minute without you will mean an eternity for me" (*R*, 137; *G*, 1:125)—are simply not acknowledged. Sentimentalities are irrelevant to the business of love making. Theobald remarks, "In the end, I think, we'll settle on a fixed day every week, for which I'll make the arrangements. . . . Otherwise your impatience could be fatal for you. If you're prepared to be content with a limited number of times, both of us will always be sure of achieving the maximum pleasure" (*R*, 137; *G*, 1:124). The other people entering Maske's sphere—Mandelstam, Scarron, and a third boarder, Stengelhöh—are conceived of as sources of money. They also give a certain pleasure to the spectator Maske: their fragile health can help to boost his ego. Mandelstam, furthermore, is to be trained to shave Maske in the mornings, which is useful. The fact that Stengelhöh suffers from constipation is, on the other hand, "strictly his own affair" (*R*, 142; *G*, 1:131).

The True Art of Unmasking

Interestingly enough, Maske applies these economic principles also vis-à-vis his two boarders. He shows no interest in lifting their masks and even seems to further their purposes of cuckolding him. Two boarders, he says, when agreeing to the contract, might be too burdensome for Luise. It is thus a nice coincidence that Scarron will use his room only during the daytime. This will allow Luise "during the day to be devoted unreservedly to Herr Scarron and for the rest of the time to Herr Mandelstam." The two boarders, in addition, should also be happy to hear that "we, my wife especially, are not averse to doing favors" (*R*, 98; *G*, 1:57).

One early critic remarked that Sternheim opens his play as if he were to embark on a cuckoldry comedy.[9] There is the middle-aged Maske, a seemingly impotent family tyrant, and his young wife Luise with a multitude of legitimate complaints. There is Fräulein Deuter, the thirty-year-old spinster, who will act as a matchmaker, and there are two lovers in the disguise of boarders. A spectator can hardly expect anything from this opening than to be treated to the delights of cuckolding, and the remarks just quoted can only reconfirm this expectation.

At the start of the second act, Mandelstam, who has become jealous of Scarron's apparent success, tries to open Maske's eyes. To no avail. Theobald refuses to listen to any hints and suggestions. Mandelstam, he declares, has fallen victim to his profession. He constantly makes up fantasty stories in order to amuse his clients and therefore can no longer distinguish between the real and the fantastic. He might even end up telling Maske that he, Mandelstam, himself, is trying to seduce Luise. A ridiculous thought. He, Maske, can be certain that his eyes see what is real, namely that Maske's basic concern is to get his numbers to agree, that Mandelstam is a hairdresser and not quite firm in the saddle, that Scarron writes love poems, and that Luise is Maske's wife.

According to the conventions of comedy, Maske's refusal to ac-
knowledge the truth would definitely expose him as the comic
fool, an object of derision. For Maske, however, the conventional
plot of a cuckold comedy would fall into the category of the extrav-
agant; such a plot has the same functions as the reports on the sea
monster or as Mandelstam's barbershop stories. They are made up
to satisfy the public's thirst for sensations. Sternheim, in a later
adaptation of Molière's *L'Avare*, reflected upon the expectations of
a normal comedy audience in the following way. The author knows
—Harpagon, the hero of the play, says there—"that all these
pleasure-seeking scandal mongers would be outraged if this pretty
youth did not prevail over the dumb wretch of a husband; if the
deceiver did not prevail over the honest man. That's the course of
action expected in this silly world. He does not have the courage to
show the extraordinary" (*G*, 2:313).

Sternheim, in *The Bloomers*, does of course have this courage.
The extraordinary lies in the simple fact that the action does not
follow literary conventions, but rather stays within the ordinary.[10]
Poets conceive the world as a stimulus to write poetry—as Scarron
does when left alone with Luise; and fantasy-loving barbers with
sickly nerves 'and an enthusiasm for Wagner's operas will idolize
women in fantastic terms or accept them as nurses—as Mandelstam
does in the course of the action. By contrast, the clerk Maske, with
his concern for the correctness of numbers, can see behind a person's mask. He can distinguish the bankrupt from the solvent and
the sound from the unsound. Mandelstam, he notices during the
theoretical discussions, "dissipates his limited resources" (*R*, 120;
G, 1:95); and he has seen at first sight that his boarders are bankrupt in physical terms. They have exhausted the energies of their
bodies and their wills. This is the only truth worth finding; and it
is a truth which lies open to the eye of anyone who can see. To do
more and to get lost in the thicket of a barber's imagination would
be a waste of Maske's resources.[11]

A Middle-Class Domestic Comedy

The dramatic genre with which the middle class conquered the
stage in the eighteenth century was the domestic or bourgeois trag-

edy. Its prototype, Lillo's *London Merchant*, shows a business apprentice who allows himself to be tempted by his sexual fantasies. The stations of his sad career are an ill-placed feeling of pity, lovemaking, moral and financial bankruptcy, murder, and the gallows. The positive hero of this genre is the *père de famille*, who tries to keep his family members away from the downward path. He has to find out, however, that his task is practically insoluble. He knows that the world outside the family, the world of the courts, of conspicuous consumption, of the pleasure houses is full of traps and temptations. Only a strict and methodical training in asceticism can shield against them. Yet, at the same time, the middle classes are beginning to discard their ascetic ideals. Their advanced economic power not only gives them access to luxury goods, but also furthers the development of—strictly speaking— luxurious moral ideals. The eighteenth-century bourgeois develops the virtues of compassion and interpersonal understanding, the ability to form ties of love and friendship. Such virtues will supposedly be the pillars of the new middle-class society;[12] to develop them, however, requires an opening of the senses and a training of imaginative faculties. The new family morality thus develops the very qualities which will be destructive to its members. It is, in Lillo's *London Merchant* and in other plays of this genre, the warm, compassionate heart which allows the enemy to intrude, and there is only one step from pity to illicit sex. Nor can anyone interfere effectively in this fatal process. Among the father's main qualities are love, trust, and understanding. With these attitudes, he is reduced to the position of an observer. He can only offer help after the catastrophe has already happened.

The fact that Sternheim called *The Bloomers* a "domestic" or "bourgeois" comedy[13] can only be seen as counterprogrammatic. Its bourgeois hero is a genuine comedy figure, and he is so for perhaps three major reasons. In contrast to his tragic counterpart, he is successful in the task of keeping his house intact. His success— and this is the second aspect to be mentioned—is based on a process of systematic psychological and perceptual reduction. Maske ignores all the ideals which the middle classes had developed in the realm of private ethics, and he stresses all those which characterize the bourgeoisie in the field of business. His ideal in life is, as he tells Luise, one of total congruence: "All the trouble in the world comes when two factors forming one entity are incongruous" (*R*, 81; *G*, 1:30). The two factors, in this case, are Luise's attractiveness and his limited salary. They are, in more general terms, the debits and assets on the page of a ledger. Other such potential debits are children, sea monsters, philosophical thoughts, psychological inquiries, the sentimentalities of love, and, finally, the curious need which some people feel to excel and to attract public attention. All such endeavors and character traits can be considered "demons who are active in our souls" (*R*, 82; *G*, 1:32).

Different from the historical bourgeois, however—and this is the third comedy feature—Maske shows no interest in long-term planning for the sake of economic profits. On the contrary, he is thoroughly hedonistic and will never decline a pleasure if it can be had for free and without further obligations. He has rid himself of the imaginary values which society offers and thus has gained the freedom to enjoy the real ones.

With all this, to be sure, *The Bloomers* presents a remarkably frivolous solution to the problems of middle-class life; and a spectator willing to appreciate Maske's competence in exploiting the freedom inherent in a limited bourgeois existence certainly needs to remember that, by its very nature, comedy tends to treat serious matters lightly. The following play, *The Strongbox*, bears the same basic characteristic. Its hero, the high-school teacher Krull, starts out as the counterfigure of the formidable Maske. In the first four acts of this comedy, Krull manages to turn everything, even money, into a stimulus for his reckless imagination. At the end of the play, however, he reaches the degree of cruel wisdom which is typical of all of Sternheim's middle-class heroes.

Chapter Four
The Strongbox
The Battle of Money and Sex

Comedy, it has been said, is tied to the rites of spring and its standard ending, the presentation of the loving couple who have overcome the obstacles put in their way by older generations—taboos and social conventions—is the delightful symbol of rejuvenation and of life's superior power. If so, Sternheim's *The Strongbox*[1] could be called an anticomedy. Twice during the play, in acts 1 and 5, a loving couple is presented. They are, however, returning from their honeymoons, not embarking on them, and their love will not bear any lasting fruit. The end of the play shows two husbands who have abandoned their young wives for the pleasures offered by a box filled with government bonds.

In tune with comic tradition, the play still presents the battle between love and money, and between young and old; but the weapons used in this fight are so uneven as to make the outcome predictable from the very beginning. The opening scenes show the newlyweds, the high school teacher Krull and his young second wife Fanny, indulging in sweet memories of their Rhine trip. Their enthusiasm is soon quenched by Fanny's aunt Elsbeth, who is the owner of the box. Elsbeth wonders about the money they must have spent and the debts they must have incurred, and she does not fail to mention the sums which they already owe her and the bank. Elsbeth does not necessarily want her money back, but she wants a good return on it and on the expectations which she has to offer. "You owe me money, you grow more obligated to me. I demand respect. . . . You want to come into my money. . . . That always calls for action" (*S*, 97–98; *G*, 1:373); "I want to enjoy my wealth. . . . I'm the one who counts in this house" (*S*, 134; *G*, 1:427).

The question as to the best use to be made of money is central to the play. For Elsbeth, the answer is obvious. It is not buying power which she is after, but rather the power which money can give her over other people. She wants a position of absolute authority in the house. Hints of the will she is going to write and the arrival of a lawyer are almost enough to ensure her victory. Her most formidable weapon, however, is the box, the visual representation of her riches. It adds a sensual element to the abstract quality of money. For Krull, the contemplation of the box thus becomes a pleasure equal to the contemplation of his wife's body, and it is not surprising that the box can easily assume Fanny's place in the couple's bedroom. If Elsbeth uses her box as a bait, Fanny presents her breasts as a symbol of pleasures to be expected. She too tries to offer them at the strategically right times. Yet to no avail. She has lost, as she says, her locket medallion on the trip. But then, it might also have slipped down her blouse. Could Krull find it for her?

KRULL: (feeling his way) I have it! (He pulls it out.) Sweet little wife, sweet. . . .
FANNY: Henry.
KRULL: The world, ah the world is beautiful! To sink. . . . (They embrace.)
(After a moment) How much might she have?
FANNY: Fifty, sixty thousand at least.
KRULL: Sixty thousand. I thought so too! (S, 99; G, 1:375)

A reader should not approach such a scene, or the play in general, with overly romantic notions in mind.[2] Fanny's relationship to her husband is not much more sentimental than is Elsbeth's. She is not in love with him but wants sexual satisfaction in return for the gifts which her body has to offer. Thus, when Krull starts sleeping with the box, she does not "bear a grudge" against him, but she is "starved" (S, 140; G, 1:439) and when she approaches her husband with the words "I love you," he can rightfully question the meaning of this phrase: "What, in the last analysis, does this constantly repeated, empty twaddle mean? You dug your fangs into my flesh to satisfy your lust—and what do you do for me, what?" (*S*, 128; *G*, 1:418). Fanny's answer to this question —"I protect you from her"—does not indicate a sufficient return for the energies which Krull needs to satisfy her. All told, Fanny's offers are no match for the fascinating qualities of money. Very soon, therefore, Krull has become Elsbeth's slave and has to give in to her most absurd whims.

This is how the action proceeds. Elsbeth has commissioned a set of portraits from the photographer Seidenschnur. On second thought, and after the pictures have already been delivered, she chooses to find them unpleasant and sends Krull out to cancel the deal (act 1). He succeeds and returns the pictures to Seidenschnur (act 2). He is then told to retrieve the pictures, of course for free. At this point, Krull has no qualms about using his wife for this mission. He sends her into Seidenschnur's bachelor apartment (act 3). Fanny complies. She finds out, however, that Seidenschnur is no more faithful a lover than Krull had been. He leaves the attractive Fanny in order to marry Lydia, Krull's daughter from a first marriage and the supposed heiress of the box (act 4); and he finally leaves both women in order to join Krull in his contemplation of the golden calf (act 5).

The Laws of Exchange and the Images of Feudalism

To a certain extent, the middle-class world presented in *The Strongbox* is again governed by the laws of exchange, by the principles of give and take, of investment and return. Theoretically, at least, it is a world of free contracts and consists only of equal partners. On the level of sexuality, this concept may even work. Fanny and Krull or Fanny and Seidenschnur can give and receive equal amounts of sensual pleasure. The relationship between Krull and Elsbeth, however, disregards these laws. They meet each other in the roles of master and slave, and they exchange real services for mere expectations. Elsbeth is well aware of this fact, and she also knows that it is not really money which makes her the master. It is not on one's riches, but "on the imagination of others," that one can "capitalize a great deal" (*S*, 144; *G*, 1:443).

Besides the laws of exchange, there is thus a second set of rules and concepts which structures the interaction of the family mem-

bers. It consists only of phantasmagorical elements. These, however, are strong enough to subjugate those who get entangled in
their web; and, more than the others, it is Krull, the head of the
family, whose actions are determined on this second level. This is
no coincidence. Within the world of free exchange, the concept of
the patriarchal family is a relic of older, feudal ages. Its head, the
father, does not legitimize his position of power through the services which he renders and the goods which he offers, but he
justifies them on the grounds of his quasi-divine position. Unlike
the businessman, the patriarchal father is not a contractor, but a
creator (of his children), a supreme protector (of the family members), and the supreme owner of everything belonging to the
house.

Krull does not have any real basis which would allow him to establish such a position; yet, in his own imagination, he still sees
himself in the role of a patriarch and, thus, of a godlike figure. At
least he does so at the beginning of the play. He considers himself
"the beginning and the end" (S, 128; G, 1:418) of all familial
matters; he thinks that he can dispense his feelings to, or withhold
them from, both women at will; and the quarrels between Elsbeth
and Fanny, their intrigues and outbursts of rage and hatred are, according to his wishful thinking, a puppet play which they produce
for his amusement: "Women! Either they realize that they perform
their stunts, easy for me to see through, for my pleasure and with
my permission, or the devil may cook them!" (S, 128; G, 1:419).
Whatever pleasure these women may offer, Krull thinks it is offered for free, and he is in a position to choose either the one or the
other without binding himself:

Ho, ho, ho! The strongbox! Each of you carries her own in lifted palms
and shows it to me from morning till night with the alluring call,
"Come, little one, come, heh-heh-heh. I've lost my locket deep down my
bosom." Ha, ha, ha. And I serve myself from it. But no hole is so deep
that I would not, going through the bottom, hit upon myself. (S, 128; G,
1:419)

Only God or his earthly replica, the absolute despot, would be
justified in making such a statement.

Krull's imagination has not only fallen victim to the myth of the patriarchal family. This myth is only part of a much larger system of symbols and metaphors. All of these are identical in at least one respect: they are borrowed from a feudal form of society as interpreted by the nineteenth-century cultural tradition. Krull's first statement on stage is, in this respect, symptomatic: "Children, all's right with God's world on a beautiful spring morning! Gliding down German rivers into the valley, proud castles salute us from on high. Germania greets you, and the Loreley, too, until on the brazen horse in Coblenz"—(*S*, 95; *G*, 1:369). Krull's perception of the world is obviously formed by the prefabricated patterns of travel brochures. These, however, feed on the cultural idols which nineteenth-century nationalism has produced. God's beautiful world is presented by the "German" river Rhine, a major symbol of nationalism. The tourist who glides down this river is surrounded by a picture world of old feudal relics—proud castles—and their modern imitations—the monument "Germania" and the "brazen horse"—by relics which appear to be as permanent as rocks and seem to be exempt from the laws of nature and history. Besides these eternal monuments of national glory and knighthood, the sentences finally refer to one further element: the demonic world of the legend, represented by the man-destroying sorceress Loreley.[3]

Krull's private world in his own house is made up of similar images. There is Fanny, his wife, who is repeatedly compared to a sorceress and vampire. She has "poisoned" Krull "to the core with love"; she intends to "swallow" him "hide and hair" (*S*, 92; *G*, 1:366); she pillages his organism (*S*, 111; *G*, 1:394); and to satisfy her lust she has "dug her fangs into his flesh" (*S*, 128; *G*, 1:418). Elsbeth is her counterpart: she is called a man-eater, a viper hissing with greed, who presses "a conglomerate of poisons into her victims" (*S*, 132; *G*, 1:424); she is a dragon trying to emasculate and devour Krull (*S*, 128; *G*, 1:419).

Thrown among such monsters, the male has to be an embodiment of heroism. Besides defending himself, he also has to act the part of the knight errant and protect the ladies in distress. It is at this point, above all, that the feudal imagery can be used to turn the self-styled master into a real slave. The hero, the "kingly man," can claim his title only as long as he performs heroic acts, and the knight errant is defined by his ability and willingness to protect others from real or imaginary perils. One only needs to think of the abundant use to which such images were put in Wilhelminian and Fascist propaganda to appreciate their effectiveness.[4] They all try to bring man into a position where he is willing to perform real, even fatal, services for the promise of mere honorary rewards.

Elsbeth's and Fanny's appeals to Krull's heroism operate, of course, on the banal level of comedy; they follow, however, the same structural line. "Be my hero as you seem to be in our nights together," Fanny pleads in order to activate Krull against Elsbeth, and continues: "I'm suffering. Liberate me, my superman, my king" (S, 106; G, 1:386). Similarly, it is Elsbeth's expectation that Krull will be a man "who will, without hesitation, "come to the defense of a well-to-do lady of the highest standing" (S, 102; G, 1: 379).

To defend this "lady of the highest standing" Krull has to solve a trivial problem. A contract involving photographs is to be canceled. In legal terms this is, as Krull points out, an unjustifiable demand. In heroic terms, matters are different, and Krull can, therefore, describe the letter which he has sent to Seidenschnur as a "breviary of thundering protest. Cutting in tone to the brink of insult" (S, 107; G, 1:387).

A business letter thus becomes a declaration of war. If Seidenschnur were a gentleman, Krull says, he would have to slap his adversary's face. A duel would ensue. Seidenschnur, who is Krull's match in matters of imaginary heroism, has a similar concept of the matter. Photographs are, for him, not objects of trade, but works of art. To see his pictures rejected would be his "Austerlitz," and to see them criticized would touch his honor; and "in matters of honor," he says, he is "sensitive to the brink of unconsciousness" (S, 104; G, 1:383).

The comic effect of such sentences is, of course, based mainly on the disparity between the high symbolic level and the trivialities it relates to. Veritable declarations of war are issued in order to save a few pennies or, at best, to save an inheritance. A reader might therefore reach the conclusion that Sternheim's comedy demonstrates not much more than the well-known fact that it is money which rules this world, and that the use of ideals and poses is nothing but an all too transparent facade. Yet such a simple distinction between reality and pretension does not do justice to the play. First of all, the heroic images can exert their power over Krull only because he thoroughly believes in them and, second, Elsbeth's box, the motivating force of Krull's actions which might be considered real, is just as imaginary as his notions of chivalry and despotic power. The box is just one, although the most important, element in the phantasmagorical web in which Krull's perception is so hopelessly entangled.

Neither Krull nor Seidenschnur are fascinated by the buying power which the box could offer them.[5] After all, they are both in a financially secure postion and earn as much as the bonds would yield in interest. In the same way, the freedom from work, the leisurely existence which the owner could enjoy, is mentioned only in passing. Seen from these two aspects, the box would yield only a small and very distant return for a big investment of energies. The essential value which Krull ascribes to the box lies on a completely different level. Its possession seems to convey a solidity which is otherwise unattainable. In this respect, the mere outside of the box is already sufficient to excite the imagination. It is a heavy solid object, and its lock has been made by a "royal locksmith" (*S*, 135; *G*, 1:429). Seidenschnur has a box too: his camera. Yet, how shaky does the latter look when compared to that "emblem of bourgeois prosperity, handed down and well established" (*S*, 155: *G*, 1:461).[6]

The content of the box is equally well chosen to excite the imagination along these lines. Different from stocks, which are dependent on the vicissitudes of the market, government bonds appear to Krull to be solid as a "rock" (*S*, 111; *G*, 1:394). Their value in this case is rooted in Bavarian forests which, again different from business enterprises, seem to come out of God's own hands and cannot be touched by revolutions or wars. Forests, furthermore, are rooted in history. Generations of foresters had to work to improve and preserve them. The possession of such values, Krull wishfully concludes, raises the owner out of the fleeting mode of existence typical for the middle classes: it gives him "roots."

The examples show that Krull's self-stylization as a medieval hero and despot, and his perception of the box, are entirely on the same level. The box can exert its influence on him only because it feeds the very fantasies after which Krull had fashioned his existence all along, and it can rank highest in his hierarchy of values only because it would seem to give his heroic dreams a basis in reality.[7]

The Real Value of Money

Since Krull is after a nobleman's existence, rooted in history and based on the unshakable value of land, he can no longer be satisfied with the simple legal concept of ownership. His ideal is to be a possessor in the emphatic sense of the word,[8] in the sense of knowing and being identical with one's belongings "down to their essence and to their last detail." It is his intent to "become a real master of his treasures down to his last drop of blood" and to investigate all his values "to the very core of their qualities" (S, 121; G, 1:409). In this way, he thinks, he will be able to give firmness to his person and achieve an unshatterable unity of the ego.[9]

This obsessive quest for the qualities of a "possessor" has a surprising result. In the course of the fourth act, Krull gradually realizes that he has been the victim of a simple illusion. Even if he were to own the box and its content, he would still be incapable of realizing his feudal dreams. The bonds which he holds in his hands remain abstractions; they do not represent Bavarian forests, but are part of the endless intertwinings and intricacies of the modern financial world. The system to which they belong defies the limits of human imagination, let alone knowledge. Thus they also shatter the concept of individual character. The owner is tied, with his financial interests, to the various, mutually exclusive and competing elements of an anarchic economic system.[10] The seeming solidarity of the box is built upon an abyss, and Krull can only be "dazzled" when he tries to investigate the bases of his fortune (S, 143; G, 1:441).

Once Krull has gained this insight, he can go through a learning process which is based on the dialectics of inner weakness and outer aggression, of the slave turning tyrant.[11] First of all, he recognizes the real profit which Elsbeth has so far drawn from her money. He, Krull, is the "essence" of her treasures (*S*, 143; *G*, 1:442); her return consists in directing and watching his comic performances, and the only question for her might be whether or not his amusing actions can be considered a four percent dividend on her capital. If this is the real value which money can convey, Krull will start the same pleasurable game for himself, if possible on an even grander scale. Elsbeth had still been modest in her demands. Krull, who has lived a humble life for forty years, will increase the percentage of his return. His greed "to exploit men for his own lust" has grown stronger than hers:

Sleepless nights do not orientate me in the least as to its real value. However, I grow strong, filled with exalted feeling, if, with the halo of prestige that property lends, I stretch out my claws into the world, toward the people, and make them dance in all humility before the chimera! (*S*, 143; *G*, 1:441)

At the end of act 3, Elsbeth had changed her will. The money will go to the church. She sees no reason to be linked to her relatives even after her death. Critics have regarded the fact that Krull will never inherit the money as one of the play's major punch lines,[12] and they have wondered why Sternheim never lets Krull find out about the testamentary change. Such thinking, however, misinterprets the intention of the play and the "real" value which Sternheim ascribes to money. As the last quotation indicates, it is not ownership, but mere appearance, which counts in this game. As long as Krull can keep the box in his room, he can easily be the master of others, for again, it is not on one's money but "on the imagination of others" that one can "capitalize a great deal."

In the fifth act, then, Krull exchanges the position of deluded victim for that of a realistic master. His victim is Seidenschnur, whom he has accepted as a son-in-law because he "smacks of romanticism" (*S*, 144; *G*, 1:443). Elsbeth has consented to the marriage for the same reason. Whatever Seidenschnur does, he will be the marionette in the hands of Krull, who will direct his movements for his own pleasure. The rules of this game are not difficult to learn. Seidenschnur returns from his honeymoon, as Krull did in the first act. Krull, therefore, only needs to repeat the lines which Elsbeth had used before. Simple words like "Aha" or "see see" or "indeed" are enough to utterly confuse this object of comic contemplation. Why, after all, Seidenschnur is asked, did Krull and Elsbeth finance his honeymoon if not for some return? Why did they accept him into the family? Seidenschnur's protestations that his liberty is being attacked are met with laughter; his outbreak: "But I wasn't born to give you pleasure" is a simple sign of immaturity. "One must be older than you," Krull retorts, "to discern the core of human relationships" (S, 147; G, 1:450).

The essence of human relationships consists in the pleasure which men give each other. This could be an acceptable and humane definition of man's social existence but for the fact that in the world of Krull and Elsbeth the production of pleasure is not based on mutual agreement. Pleasure is derived here only from directing and observing the comic performances of others. Seen from this aspect, however, the entire comic action appears in a new light. Krull's encounters with Seidenschnur, his alternate gestures of rage and submission, his lewdness in front of the box, the scenes which show him sleepwalking with his imaginary treasure: all these comic scenes had been produced and staged by Elsbeth. "Perfect timing" (S, 135; G, 1:429), she says at one point, alluding to her arrangement of the comic plot.

It is evident that comedy, at this point, turns into a *vision du monde*, into a new version of the old *theatrum mundi* concept. Society is a play, and each of its members assumes the role of either spectator or director or actor. The slave is he who has to perform for others; the wise man will seek the position which earlier ages have ascribed to the gods: he will direct or simply contemplate the game.

This game concept offers one further variation which the first two comedies had not yet explored. The actor need not necessarily be a victim. He can be a winner in the game if he manages to write his own script and if he can convince his spectators that he is a true-to-life hero, not a comic fool as they might have expected. *Paul Schippel Esq.* and *The Snob*, the two plays following *The Strongbox*, deal with this particular variation of the game of representation. The central figures of both plays represent the con-man type of the social climber. They both have realized that cultural idolatry constitutes one of the major weaknesses of their social environment. This means that they can achieve almost anything in life as long as they impress others by a continuous display of traits which in twentieth-century middle-class society can be called "heroic."

Chapter Five

Comedies of Social Climbing

Paul Schippel Esq.

"Le Prolétaire Bourgeois" and "O Täler weit o Höhen," the tentative titles of the play eventually called *Paul Schippel Esq.*,[1] well illustrate its ambivalent structure. The first title clearly alludes to Molière's comedy *Le Bourgeois Gentilhomme*[2] and thus introduces a new theme into Sternheim's work. The hero of the play, Paul Schippel, is a social climber who starts out as a *déclassé* and ends up as a reputable member of the middle classes. The second title, "O Täler weit o Höhen," is the first line of a well-known German folksong. From this second standpoint, the play is a further variation on themes pursued in the two previous comedies: it portrays the cultural aspirations of the middle classes, represented in this case by the cultivation of the German Lied and the widespread institution of the *Männergesangverein*.

The central figure among the burghers of the play, the goldsmith Hicketier, has all the prerequisites for an unshakably solid position. His existence is rooted in history—the Hicketiers have been goldsmiths since the Thirty Years War. By dint of his profession he is king among artisans; he is influential within his town and the undisputed master of the burghers appearing on stage. The town he lives in is the capital of a petty principality, and some of its inhabitants belong to a class superior to his own. Yet this fact in itself need not shatter his self-esteem. Hicketier's relations with the nobility are not competitive. He would, as he says, abhor a nobleman's friendship, for he likes his "spheres well defined, above and below" (*R*, 35; *G*, 1:485).

The center of his sphere, his house, is a further emblem of this solidarity: "Look at the way that house spreads itself over the face of the earth," Hicketier's antagonist Schippel, who is nothing but a destitute small-scale musician, says admiringly:

They are fleecing us for every square foot we inhabit. Here a carriage standing empty has an acre to itself. . . . No wind'll ever whistle through that, [pointing at the house:] walls about two feet thick. Inside bloated portraits of father and grandfather: Born 1836, died 1886. I haven't the former, far less the latter. (*R*, 58; *G*, 1:523)

No less solid, no less measurable in cubic feet, is the physical appearance of the Hicketiers. For Schippel it is, among other things, the goldsmith's imperious belly which utterly fascinates him; and with the same envious admiration he contemplates the appearance of Hicketier's younger sister, Thekla. He, Schippel, can hardly fill out his pants. The girl's skirt, on the other hand, is "stretched over her hips to the point of bursting" (*R*, 58; *G*, 1:523).

All outward signs point to the fact that Hicketier could be the replica of the unshatterable Maske. As opposed to the clerk, however, the goldsmith is not satisfied with "real" values. "It's in his nature," his wife Jenny says about him, "to need symbols" (*R*, 27; *G*, 1:471). He has surrounded himself with a set of images, with products of his imagination which obscure his sense of reality and cause his defeat. There is, as the first symbol to be mentioned, Hicketier's sister. Although past the age of adolescence, she still has to enact the part of pure innocence and virginal chastity in order to keep intact her brother's poetic view of the world. The second symbol, the one central to the plot, is a wreath, the prize of a singing contest which Hicketier and his friends Wolke and Krey have already won twice. To win it again and thus to keep it permanently has been their "dearest dream" since childhood. To give it up would be the tragedy of their lives. Symbols, furthermore, are not only the goals of their endeavors; most of their interactions take on symbolic forms as well. Simple agreements are enacted in the form of oaths reminiscent of David's famous painting *The Oath of the Horatii*; steps taken toward gaining the wreath are reported in terms of heroic battle; relationships between men and women become comparable to those of minstrels being consumed by their love or are fashioned after the model of shepherdesses professing their hearts' desires to the wind.

Where such self-tailored symbols do not suffice, outside forces provide the imagination with more food. The prince is the first

one to abuse the burghers' fantasies in this way. He could not care
less about wreaths and songs, but he has cast an eye on Thekla,
and he knows that he will reach his goal more easily if he can keep
Hicketier busy with preparations for the singing contest:

> PRINCE (to himself): Something as amusing as this so close at hand and
> one is consumed by blackest boredom. (Aloud) The male choir; a thing of
> major importance and close to the hearts of the people demands our
> closest consideration, a worthy weapon against the onslaughts of an age
> without ideals. The German *Lied*, gentlemen! In this regard we shall take
> extraordinary measures, grace the forthcoming festival with our princely
> presence. (To himself) Heavens, what am I saying. (*R*, 39; *G*, 1:491).

"The German *Lied* against anarchy" (*R*, 40; *G*, 1:492)—this is
how Wolke interprets the prince's improvised speech uncovering,
in this way, one hidden motif of his own cultural aspirations. It is
through symbols, through activities on the cultural level, that
these burghers try to maintain their social identity and fend off the
"anarchistic" attacks from the lower ranks of society. It is their dilemma and the play's major irony that it is this very strategy
which makes them vulnerable to attack.

Hicketier's hopes that he would be able to keep his "spheres
well defined" are shattered in the third act. The prince, the in-
truder from above, attains an easy victory over Hicketier's sister
Thekla. Princes are prominent figures in many folksongs and thus
also in Thekla's dreams. She is therefore more than willing to be
seduced by such a quasi-poetical human being. The second in-
truder, the one from below, is Schippel, the destitute musician,
who bears the additional stigma of an illegitimate birth. Yet the
burghers cannot do without him. He is the only qualified tenor in
town; with him the wreath will be won, without him it will be
lost. Hicketier's plan is to hire him, or rather his voice, for a fee
and to keep all relations with this social outcast on the level of a
business transaction. It is Schippel's "vocal material" (*R*, 47; *G*,
1:504) which he is after, a commodity which he thinks he can buy
like everything else. In the fourth act, after Thekla's transgression,
Hicketier even plans to put his dealings with Schippel on a larger
scale. The deflowered girl needs a husband and Schippel is to fill

the need. His reward in this transaction will be Thekla's consider-able dowry.

Schippel's reactions to such business propositions seem, at first sight at least, contradictory. In the first act, he refuses the deal. He is not interested in money but in social acceptance. In the terms of comic interaction, he wishes to be close to others, to grab them by their vest buttons, to pat their bellies, to shake their hands; in more socially acceptable terms, he expects to be talked to in public and to be invited to the burghers' houses. Hicketier, however, considers this too high a price for a voice and a wreath, and he calls the deal off. By the time the opponents meet again, Schippel seems to have changed his mind. He offers his voice for free, but he also accepts some money. Yet, as it turns out, Schippel has only temporarily changed strategies. In the third act, and prior to Thekla's affair with the prince, he asks for Thekla's hand but finds himself confronted with Hicketier's unrestrained fury. The next and essential turnabout occurs in the fourth act. Hicketier now offers Thekla of his own free will; he does not re-frain, however, from alluding to her affair. Now, it is Schippel's turn to call the deal off, and he does so in the snarling tone of voice which a Prussian lieutenant would have used in his refusal to marry the girl whom he had dishonored.

SCHIPPEL: Don't think that my well-rooted concept of manly honor will allow me to press my suit further.
HICKETIER (in consternation): What?!
SCHIPPEL: I think not. I will have to reserve my decision. (*R*, 67; *G*, 1:538)

Many critics have shared Hicketier's consternation. Schippel, they have concluded, is at this point just another victim of middle-class fantasies.[3] A more careful reading of the text can, however, easily refute such interpretations.[4] From beginning to end, Schippel pur-sues only one goal—social integration—and the seeming turn-abouts of his actions are nothing but adequate reactions to changed situations. It is evident that a mere business relationship with the burghers will not further Schippel's plans. He cannot sell anything but himself. Vis-à-vis Hicketier, he is thus in the position of a real proletarian: he can be the formally free partner in an economic transaction only if he consents to being, at the same time, the object of trade. The deal which Hicketier proposes in the fourth act does not alter this situation. Here again, Schippel's person is made the object of trade and—what is more—of ridicule.[5] The goods which Schippel is allowed to acquire are flawed. Schippel would be, in Hicketier's own words, a "rag-man" who has to content himself with other people's throwaways.

Quite understandably, then, Schippel has to refrain from getting involved in simple business transactions, and he further has to be careful not to be assigned the part of the comic fool. There is, then, only one strategy left for him, namely, to play the part of the hero instead. Heroism, in middle-class terms, can be defined as a willingness to act for the sake of sublime principles only, without any regard for material rewards. The hero is a person who will sacrifice anything, if necessary his life, in the pursuit of some ideal.

Schippel, in a climactic series of actions, proves to be such a hero. If in the first act he still demands a price for his voice, he seems, in the second act, willing to offer it for free. He has memorized the prince's proclamation about the contest, the cultural importance of which is now deeply engraved in his mind. This sudden sensitivity is more than it takes to shatter Hicketier's concept of the world. The mere fact that Schippel can sing at all must already confuse him. It was his expectation that "despite fine vocal material" Schippel's low background would not permit him to grasp "the historical importance of the prize song" (R, 47; G, 1:504). It is his belief, furthermore, that the ability to sing is part of a well-settled bourgeois existence. Hence his bewilderment: "Such melody from that proletarian breast! Not cracked or shaky the way the lower class sing, but aware of the universal harmony of all being" (R, 57; G, 1:522).

Schippel's voice alone is thus a blow to Hicketier's self-esteem. He receives his second blow when Schippel discovers his "manly honor" and refuses to marry Thekla without, however, giving up his efforts to win the wreath. The third and final act of heroism occurs at the end of the play. It takes on the form of a duel between Schippel and Thekla's husband Krey, who has to defend his wife's honor from certain hints uttered by Schippel. Schippel is realistic enough to consider the risks of this heroic enactment, and he would have run away if one of his seconds had not dragged him onto the battlefield. Fortunately, his opponents have not noticed any of this. Their own duelist is close to a nervous breakdown as well. Since neither opponent has ever fired a shot before, no serious harm is caused. Even with its flaws, however, the duel is a high point in Hicketier's life. It is an "image" which he can treasure among his most glorious memories.

Schippel, who was the major participant in this heroic ritual, will now be integrated into the middle class. He is promised his full share of all its "higher blessings" (*R*, 76; *G*, 1:553), and Hicketier, who in the first act had refused to shake this beggar's hand, will now meet him as an honorable person: "Filled with spiteful prejudice and conscious distaste for your background, I have hitherto refused you entry to our preserves. You have beaten me. I consider it a duty to tell you how much I shall be honored by your company in the future" (*R*, 76; *G*, 1:552).

There can be no doubt after such words that Schippel will be allowed to climb the ladder of success in the bourgeois world. In fact, he reappears in a later play, *Tabula Rasa*, this time as the director of a large industrial company. In this role he is confronted with another lower class figure, the blue-collar worker Ständer. Ständer shares many of Schippel's characteristics: his determination to reach his goals, his cunning, his unbroken spontaneity, and his hedonistic sensuousness. All these are traits which the anarcho-aestheticist Sternheim considered typically "proletarian." *Tabula Rasa*, however, differs from *Paul Schippel Esq*. in at least one significant aspect, thus indicating an important change in Sternheim's political and social thinking. Schippel's central goal in life, integration into middle-class society, is Ständer's major nightmare. Instead, the proletarian—and his author—now praise the freedom of an anarchical existence, one which can be enjoyed only outside the limits of middle-class society.

The Snob

Sternheim's next play, *The Snob*,[6] again presents the act of social climbing, this time on a higher level. The play's hero, Christian Maske, son of Theobald, comes from a petty bourgeois background. He has, however, been able to work his way up and, at the beginning of the play, he is already the co-founder of a mining company, one of its major share holders, and its future director. All of this means that he has now reached a point in his career where his former middle-class attitudes will no longer suffice. Key positions in politics as well as in business are still in the hands of the nobility. Its members, though lacking in economic power, influence the cultural atmosphere which prevails among business magnates. In order to reach his goal and be unreservedly accepted within the higher circles, Christian must impress through impeccably aristocratic qualities. In addition, he has to redefine the rules which determine his conduct.

Unlike the bourgeois, the aristocrats define their own lives in terms of stagecraft. They are not allowed the privacy and anonymity which the middle classes enjoy; instead, their actions are recorded in the annals of their families, and they have to live their lives under the ever-watchful eyes of their clan and of the public. In becoming the director of a company, Christian will be a public person himself. Henceforth he will have to combine the cleverness of the bourgeois with an aristocratic air of distinction; his maneuvers will have to conform to the principles of both profitability and stagecraft.

Christian's opponent in this game is a certain Graf Palen, the head of an old but poor aristocratic family. Palen's self-esteem is based on nothing but a set of cultural beliefs. He believes that "the feeling for the values of finer taste" can be acquired only by a long process of "careful cultivation" and that this "feeling" is especially important at times when the emphasis put on financial wealth or "the brutal truth of figures demands an important counterbalance" (*R*, 162; *G*, 1:162).

In *Paul Schippel Esq.* it was the German *Lied* which had to serve as a bastion against anarchism; now aristocratic mannerisms serve

much the same function against the advance of the bourgeoisie.
Only on this level the symbols of cultural excellence are more sub-
tle. The true nobleman, though conscious of his superiority, has to
refrain from any vulgar showmanship. He knows that "on the basis
of certain of our inherited peculiarities, now part and parcel of our
nature, the inconspicuously uniform is the correct thing" (*R*, 162;
G, 1:162). Such correct behavior, he further argues, cannot be
learned. It is a quasi-inherited trait, the product of a long historical training process. Members of the middle classes can, of course,
get hold of enormous riches, they can acquire certain aristocratic
manners and beliefs. They can, however, never. fully "possess"
them. Possession, Palen explains, is an etymological derivative of
sitting,[7] and it is only through prolonged "sitting" that one can
attain the status of the true possessor. Where this tradition is
lacking, the attempts to display aristocratic manners have to remain on the level of imitation. Furthermore, a parvenu imitator
will act according to aristocratic norms only with specific goals in
mind; his movements follow the law of rational calculations and
are therefore predictable. A "possessor," on the other hand, follows
his nature and is a source of perpetual aesthetic surprises.

Within the ideological current of anticapitalistic conservativism
such thoughts were quite en vogue in the late Wilhelminian period, and reactionary political parties as well as a goodly number
of middle-class writers would have subscribed to similar tenets. It
is quite likely that Sternheim himself, with his well-known dandyish attitudes, shared some of Palen's beliefs.[8] On the other hand,
the play clearly shows the specific interest which Palen pursues in
making such statements. His philosophy is the last line of defense
for his endangered social position. "Should this man reveal that it
is not necessary to have had ancestors in order to possess certain in-
estimable values," he says, "I am denied justification in my own
eyes" (*R*, 166; *G*, 1:170). Or, as he puts it earlier: "I have been
observing him for two years. . . . If this bourgeois is really following his nature, in living our life, what difference is there between
him and us?" (*R*, 165; *G*, 1:169). It must be in Palen's interest,
therefore, to unmask the would-be aristocrat Christian as a simple
parvenu; and conversely, it is in Christian's interest to play his

game so well that the aristocrat will be full of admiration and consider him not only his social peer but also a totally desirable son-in-law.

It is the joyful message of this comedy that a good con man can outplay an aristocrat. Christian has already learned the particulars of good manners from his girl friend Sybil. The last lesson which he has to learn is how to bind his tie correctly, a feat which is accomplished simply by cutting off the loose ends. This is a wasteful procedure which contradicts all the principles of bourgeois economics; yet, in terms of stagecraft it is a necessity. It ensures the respect of the experts and it fulfills Palen's first requirement: inconspicuous uniformity.

Meeting Palen's second requirement—unquestionable distinction—is not all that difficult either. If examined closely, the concept of distinction is void of any specific meaning and he who, in one way or another, deviates from the norm can already be considered distinguished.[9] Thus, on a banal level, even an inadvertent faux pas may do. Christian once addresses Palen in the humble form of "Herr Graf" where "Graf" would have been correct; and he is praised by the count for his awareness of "nuances."

This unique relevance of style, poses, and theatrical effectiveness governs the hero's actions throughout the play. Christian calculates his appearance in the same way as the manager of a political campaign calculates every step which his candidate takes. Should he appear alone or should he be in the midst of an entourage? Should he present himself as a self-made man and outsider or should he pose as the legitimate heir of an honorable tradition? These are the questions which Christian has to consider; and he knows that there are no general rules to this game. The fancies of his spectators are as unpredictable as the conditions of the market. That which was shocking yesterday may be admirable today and boring tomorrow. The game of conmanship, in other words, has to be played by ear and with a close eye on the public. On the other hand, it is this very unpredictability of taste and fancies which makes it easy to come up with surprises to appear "aloof and mysterious" (R, 173; G, 1:181), and thus to refute Palen's belief that a middle-class parvenu can be found out because his actions are always calculated.

Only one difficulty remains: whatever part Christian chooses to play and however he wishes to stage himself, he must deliver his lines with grand gestures and with the appearance of utmost conviction. He must give up the belief that a human character constitutes a unity. Christian's character at least can be nothing but a simple function of fluctuating situations and of changing strategies.

Such simple deviations from the norm are, however, not sufficient in the long run. Christian knows that it is not enough to be unpredictable; he must be admirable and he must baffle his observers by ever new fireworks. He also knows that for this purpose he must overcome his bourgeois inclination to choose the easy way and his preference for the economy of means and goals. He has, for instance, received a letter from Palen inviting him to a private dinner party. Christian's goal is to marry Palen's daughter Marianne, and to accept the invitation would, of course, seem to further his plans. Yet, he also knows that his answering letter will be considered his first "public statement" and that it will have to be "significant." The problem is "what four or five syllables can make me seem important for a moment to minds like theirs" (*R*, 152: *G*, 1:147). The opening word which Christian finally chooses for this letter is impressive in its length and in its rhythm. It forces him, however, to decline the invitation. Yet, in such a case, content is irrelevant when compared to style.

At the beginning of the play, for his first appearance in public, it seems most effectual for Christian to pose alone. An entourage would allow his spectators to compare him with others and would reduce him to normal size. Family, background, any suggestions of the hero's past have to be discarded. Christian succeeds in ridding himself of the relics of his past life by defining them in business terms. His parents and his girl friend have invested money and energy in him: they are his creditors. Christian is now in a position to close his accounts with his father and mother by paying off the advance plus interest. They are sent to Switzerland to prevent the possibility of further embarrassment. Sybil is paid off in a similar way, and her status is changed from friend to paid mistress.[10]

Once the personality had been admired for his unique qualities, his manager can afford to reduce him in size and to make the public acquainted with some of the more common features of his character. Christian follows this theatrical principle in the second act. Social customs have changed anyway. It has become fashionable to pose as the prodigious son of "poorly, but cleanly dressed parents." Or, as Palen puts it: "Such simple origins can make personal merit stand out all the more, as the Emperor, our Supreme Leader, reminded us again recently" (R, 170: G, 1:176). In this situation, Christian can activate another potential facet of his ego, "his simple childlike instincts" (R, 182: G, 1:193), and he can recall his father Theobald to the scene. He knows, however, that this is a risky maneuver since he had, in the first act, declared his family dead. To allay any possible suspicions he will therefore dramatize his father's appearance on stage by presenting him "with a grand gesture as something exceptional" (R, 181; G, 1:192).

The third act, the wedding night, is the climax in this game of showmanship. Christian is afraid that his bride Marianne may still have condescending feelings toward him as a parvenu. He interprets every whisper, every giggle as an affront to himself. Marianne's maid is a viper "opening all the valves" into Marianne's "blood stream." Christian, therefore, plans to "cleanse" his wife's blood from this "poison down to the very last drop" (R, 183; G, 1:199). Cleansing somebody's blood is a metaphor which Sternheim normally uses to describe the effect which comedy has on the public. The same is true here. Before Christian can take his wife to bed, he has to enact a drama for her in which his is the part of the hero. Marianne, the spectator, "shall on this solemn evening feel and savor boundless awe. She must collapse and sprawl full length at my feet—no less" (R, 186; G, 1:203).

After a lengthy and boring speech about his economic and, above all, his political importance as an industrial magnate, Christian presents his major stage prop in this drama, a Renoir painting of a young woman which he says is a portrait of his mother. A viscount, so he tells Marianne, was present when the picture was made, approximately a year before his birth. Marianne, hearing about the viscount and the date of Christian's birth, infers more than the hero had intended. The final scene is the great celebration of devotion which Christian had planned:

MARIANNE (with outstretched arms before the picture): Sweet mother adultress! (To Christian, collapsing slowly at his feet) My dear husband and lord! (Christian's smile and grand gesture of relief.) (*R*, 193; *G*, 1:214)

Sternheim's audience, it must be added, reacted to the hero's "grand gesture of relief" with undisguised indignation. If Christian's cunning could elicit a certain amount of sympathy up to the end of the second act, his final breach of filial piety toward his own mother exceeded the limits of the spectators' tolerance. Once again the playwright Sternheim blatantly disregarded the moral feelings of his middle-class public, a provocation that was undoubtedly intentional.

In the second act, Sternheim mirrors his hero's relationship to the public by confronting him with his girl friend Sybil. Christian is about to recall his parents while Sybil—acting as a spokesman for familial piety—considers this an outrageous plan. Whatever benefit Christian may derive from presenting his father, the price will be too high: old Maske, she thinks, will become an object of general derision within his son's new surroundings. Sybil's last action in the play is to denounce the hero in the name of morality. "Oh for a word—I'd give my life to find it—one word to characterize you and express how base I find you" (*R*, 174: *G*, 1:182). She intends to join the Social Democratic party and become a critic of the likes of Maske and of capitalistic society in general.[11] For the hero, on the other hand, this last confrontation with his former girl friend is a final proof of how far behind he has already left middle-class conventions and middle-class thinking. It is time, he concludes, to burn the bridges, to make of himself a "picture, a juicy image" and to ignore his name calling audience (*R*, 174; *G*, 1:182).

The significance of this scene goes well beyond its specific function in the play. Burning bridges, abandoning lines of communication, discarding common moral standards, eliminating the usual concepts which determine man's actions: these decisions on Christian's part also characterize, as the following chapter will show, Sternheim's process of writing. His plays present comic heroes who are possessed by their goals, who have learned to present themselves in dramatic poses, and who act as if the world were a theater. Sternheim clearly sided with these heroes. They are, to quote again the words of Sternheim's preface from 1918, model figures insofar as they do "not listen to traditional roundelays" and pay no heed "to the names which middle class mentality might give to their somewhat brutal tinge of character" (G, 6:47).

Yet Sternheim leaves his spectators free to draw their own conclusions about the actions presented, and they have invariably decided against the author and his heroes. They have preferred Sybil to Christian, the moral commentator to the immoral actor or—in more general terms—they have opted, as the next chapter will show, for a satirical interpretation of Sternheim's plays and against a concept of comedy which attempts to ignore moral concerns.

Chapter Six

The Style and Function of Comedy

Forms of Theatrical Perception

To present the invisible in visual terms is probably the most basic problem faced by twentieth-century playwrights from naturalism to the present day. The art of theater depends on the visibility and the representational character of social life. Modern capitalistic societies, on the other hand, are determined by ever-increasing series of abstractions. The economic processes of production, distribution, and consumption, the mechanisms which lead to political decisions, the breakdown of small and visible social units, the dissociation of the individual into a variety of social roles and psychic layers: all these phenomena can be described in scientific terms; they might be grasped in the discursive form of the novel; they transcend, however, the technical possibilities of the stage.[1] Consequently, the dramatic genres have, for the last hundred years, lived through an almost continuous state of crisis and experimentation, and playwrights have repeatedly attempted to find a way to bridge the gap between the medium of theater and a scientifically advanced perception of reality.

The comedies discussed so far seem to defy this general observation. They are virtually free of technical experiments, and their author never seems to have questioned the ability of the theater to capture the essence of modern social life. Quite on the contrary. Sternheim repeatedly compared the stage with a mirror capable of reproducing reality if only the playwright refrained from embellishing the reflection.[2] At the most, he wrote, the dramatist has to focus his spotlight on specific aspects of social reality which are generally hidden from public view. According to Sternheim, it is one of the major achievements of his works that they deal with "average things" and that they discuss the "marginal with a zeal and an emphasis which had never before been applied to the bourgeois world."[3]

Such sentences do not, as might be assumed, express a naively realistic theory of the arts. Rather they protest against prevailing literary conventions and, at the same time, they reflect Sternheim's own conscious and deliberate efforts to overcome the problem of abstraction. As an art collector, a palace owner, and a dandy, Sternheim had already concentrated on those aspects of reality which are immediately accessible to the senses. As a playwright he did the same or even more: he tried to construct his plays in a way which virtually reverses the normal relationship between the perceptual and the underlying conceptual facets of reality.

It is a common and reasonable assumption that man's actions need to be explained in terms of hidden psychological traits, that individual phenomena can only be adequately perceived when related to general categories, and that they are real only as elements of abstract systems. More often than not, that which is visible is thus assumed to function as a mere facade hiding the essential. In the comic world of Sternheim's plays the opposite is true. Theobald Maske's dogged attempt to keep the "wall papers of his existence" sealed is meant to give him protection. At the same time, it provides the playwright with an opportunity to present Maske's three-bedroom apartment as if it were a cosmos in itself. A whole world is contained within its four walls and thus within a sphere which can be directly presented on the stage. Within this sphere, furthermore, Theobald need not show any concern for the possible reason and the hidden motivations which may have led his boarders into his apartment. The truth about them lies in their fragile physical and psychic constitution, and as such it is immediately accessible to anyone who can see. If it is hidden to the likes of Mandelstam and the normal spectator, then only because they have acquired the habit of speculating about reality rather than seeing it. Krull's learning process in *The Strongbox* can be described in similar terms. Krull learns that the "real value" of Elsbeth's money lies in the power which it gives her over others, a fact which was openly visible from the very beginning. He further realizes that in his middle-class surroundings substance is irrelevant. The appearance of riches alone is sufficient to convey power. Schippel and Christian Maske, the heroes of the following plays, make use of this very same insight on their roads toward success.

The truth is visible and lies on the surface of appearances: this eminently theatrical principle[4] of perception marks, in Krull's case, the end of a learning process. In the case of the author, it marks the end of a deliberate and methodical process of poetic transformation. The manuscripts of *Paul Schippel Esq.*, for instance, clearly show that Sternheim started writing his plays more in the mode of a conventional novelistic narrator than in compliance with the laws of theater.[5] The first version of this comedy starts with a lengthy and rather inept exposition in which the audience is provided with socio-psychological explanations of Hicketier's cultural aspirations and even with a suggestion as to the most appropriate attitude with which to watch the play. An abundance of further explanatory scenes keeps the audience informed throughout the play about the antagonists' goals and strategies and about their fears and hopes. The visible part of the world presented here is indeed only a surface layer.

In the final version of the play, Sternheim reduced these non-visual elements to a bare minimum. There is no longer a mediator between the audience and the play, but rather the comic world has become a self-contained autonomous unity which the audience confronts without any guidance or commentaries. The initial attempt to explain Hicketier's character in the light of psychological determinants is replaced by a mere definition of his character: "His very nature requires symbols." The character thus becomes a given fact. Similarly, where Schippel, in the first version, had acted as a psychologist and schemer, where he had been lost in reflections and thus had shown his inner psychic dimensions, he is now presented as a thoroughly sensuous and spontaneous character. More than by words and thoughts, he is guided by appetites, by his ability and his urges to smell, to feel, and to touch. He registers Thekla Hicketier more by her perfume than by anything else, and social acceptance now means the permission to be physically close to others: to shake their hands, to pat their bellies, to leaf through their picture books, to relax on their sofas, to peek into their bedrooms, to burp in their presence. This emphasis both on Hicketier's immutable character and on Schippel's immediate sensual drives allows Sternheim to reduce very drastically the importance of verbal means of communication, an observation which is true for all of Sternheim's successful plays. In many scenes of his comedies the spoken word functions as an accompaniment or as a simple equivalent of gestures and scenic arrangements. Sternheim's plays, in other words, show certain similarities to the silent movies of the same period[6] or, in terms of theatrical history, they can be said to revive the techniques and perceptual structures of the farce.[7]

Sternheim's Use of Language

Dramatic gestures are significant more for their expressive than for their communicative function. By exposing psychic features which are normally invisible to the eye, they also cut short any questions and speculations concerning hidden motifs and inner feelings. A person who indulges in grand gestures tries to give himself the air of an unsplit character who is beyond the usual distinction between surface appearance and inner truth.

The verbal elements in Sternheim's plays serve much the same functions. Sternheim's heroes act as if the narrow spheres of their living room were a stage and as if their conversations were part of a forensic debate in which every word carries the weight of a public announcement. No matter how private the situation and how trivial the subject matter, the *dramatis personae* will always speak in definitive and apodictic terms. That which would normally be a relaxed conversation is thus transformed into a heated debate; vague utterances are delivered with aplomb, and simple feelings are raised to the level of sublime ecstasy: "Schon hängt im Grau Ihrer Häuslichkeit zuviel Sehnsucht am Fenster und schaut aus" ("In your domestic greyness there's already too much longing that leans at the window looking out," *R*, 90; *G*, 1:44). This is the manner in which Luise Maske is informed by Fräulein Deuter that her sexual frustrations have not gone unnoticed. When Scarron asks Luise to grant his most tender wishes, he uses a similar style: "Ich bin eine Kirchenglocke. Mein Strang hängt gelähmt. Schlagen Sie mich an, so läute ich Ihrer Kehle helle Schreie" ("I am a church bell. My rope is hanging limp. If you strike me, I shall echo your throat's clear cries," (*R*, 88; *G*, 1:41). A present-day reader can easily pinpoint the model which these two speakers follow in their sentences. Syntactical and metaphorical structures such as "Sehnsucht hängt am Fenster" or "Ich läute Ihrer Kehle helle Schreie" are reminiscent of the poetic language which was just then being developed by expressionist writers. Sternheim parodies the tendencies of this literary movement from the very beginning and he does so for both aesthetic and ideological reasons. The ecstasies of expressionist language seemed to him no more than the latest attempt on the part of the middle classes to escape into the realm of fantasy. In Sternheim's second comedy, *The Strongbox*, it is Seidenschnur, the representative of the younger generation, who avoids a confrontation with reality by indulging in expressionist exaltations.[8] His "predecessor" Krull tries to do the same; he works, however, within a different metaphorical system: "140.000 Mark sind in mein Hirn geätzt und drücken auf die Waage der Entschliessungen" ("One hundred and forty thousand marks are etched into my brain and weigh down the scales of decision," *S*, 134; *G*, 1:428); "Nicht Niedrigkeit der Gesinnung ist, concidiere ich ihn [i.e., the pleasures which Elsbeth demands], doch Vernunft, Einordnung in Weltgesetze" ("It is not, if I concede it, baseness of sentiment but intelligence, adaptation to universal laws," *S*, 134; *G*, 1:427). The speaker of the first sentence might be a monarch who, in the midst of his courtly entourage, weighs his choices in the face of some supreme power. In the second sentence, it is the language of eighteenth-century middle-class philosophy which structures the line of argumentation. If the world is a rational system, reason demands that man submit to its laws. Yet it is only the would-be family tyrant Krull who speaks here, and the supreme and rational power which he confronts is only his whimsical and tyrannical aunt Elsbeth.

Examples of this nature abound in Sternheim's plays. They occur with particular frequency in the speeches of Theobald's opponents in *The Bloomers*, they prevail in the first part of *The Strongbox*, and they can be found throughout *Paul Schippel Esq.* They are relatively scarce, however, in *The Snob*. For Sternheim, the use of hollow metaphors was characteristic neither of bourgeois pragmatists nor of the nobility. It was typical, however, for middle-class megalomaniacs who tried to gain an heroic stature through the frenzied compilation of prefabricated fantasies. This frenzy is noticeable in all the above sentences. The metaphors which the speakers use are disjointed and incoherent. Their useless attempts to impress themselves and others invariably lead to nonsensical pomposity.

At first sight, such observations only seem to illustrate once more that which is generally considered the major theme and intention of Sternheim's plays. The contradiction between reality and pretense, between logic and fantasy exposes the would-be hero as a comic fool and thus serves satirical purposes. Up to a certain point, this conclusion is certainly correct. In a number of scenes, Sternheim uses the old comedy technique of confronting stylistic bombast with a sober use of language, and in all such cases he directs the public's laughter against those who have gotten lost in images. His critique of language patterns and his critique of social behavior are thus in prefect agreement.

And yet, this straightforward satirical interpretation is valid only within limits. Exaltation of language and gestures also characterizes man's attempt to act out his personality, an attempt which Sternheim considers anything but reprehensible. It is not coincidental, therefore, that Schippel, the proletarian upstart, also in- dulges in highly metaphorical statements when he describes the sudden awakening of his energies, appetites, and desires. His development from a social nonentity into a dramatic hero is indicated by a similar development in his use of language. To some extent, this observation can be generalized. Pomposity of language, one might say, has at least two distinct functions within Sternheim's plays. It is a stimulus for derision and, at the same time, a means of theatrical transformation. It allows Sternheim to present the mediocre petty bourgeois as a *dramatis persona* and to raise banality to the level of high—even though comical—drama:

Du bist die Schönste, die mir erschien. Gewitter erwarte ich von dir, Entladung, die meine letzten Erdenreste schmilzt, und in den Wahnsinn enteilend, will ich meinen entselbsteten Balg zu deinen aufgehobenen Füssen liebkosen.

You are the most beautiful woman I have ever set eyes on. I await the moment when you will unleash a storm which will break over me and demolish my mortal remains, and from the refuge of my madness I shall offer up my empty self tenderly at your feet. (*R*, 110; *G*, 1:78)

This is how the poet Scarron initiates a love scene whose climax, however, is only the production of a lyrical poem. Theobald courts his wife Luise as well. He does so, however, in the following terms: "Jetzt kann ich es, dir ein Hind zu machen, verant worten." ("For making you pregnant I can now assume responsibility," *R*, 143; *G*, 1:133). The stylistic difference between these two sentences is striking. On the one hand, a fireworks of metaphors; on the other, a barrenness of style which can help to explain why one critic called Sternheim the "least poetic" among contemporary playwrights.[10] Unpoetic: this may indeed be an adequate characterization of the language used by such heroes as Theobald, Elsbeth Treu, and Christian Maske. And yet their sentences are anything but a simple copy of everyday colloquial German. The model figures of Sternheim's plays are engaged in drama as much as their opponents, and their statements have a highly theatrical and heroic quality of their own. Only, in this case, this quality originates from a rather unlikely source: from the form of communication used in bureaucratic letters, in legal writs, or in statements as they might be exchanged between an irate tenant and his landlord or between a bank and its negligent debtor. Sternheim's heroes, one could say, phrase their sentences as if they were engaged in some pretrial hearing. They seem to live on the verge of a civil suit, possibly the most dramatic event in a normal middle class existence.

In act 3 of *The Strongbox*, the deluded patriarch Krull reports to Elsbeth that he has settled the nasty business with Seidenschnur's photographs. He is in a state of exaltation, and his report abounds in metaphors and poetic images and thus makes Elsbeth suspicious of the reliability of his statements. Her ensuing question would be

unremarkable only if it were used by a district attorney confronting
an unreliable subordinate: "Du bist nicht bei Trost. Hat deine
Versicherung, Seidenschnur verzichtet, in solchem Zustand
abgegeben, überhaupt Wert" ("You are not in your right mind.
Your assurances that Seidenschnur renounces are they, stated in
such a condition, of any validity?" *S*, 130; *G*, 1:421). When
Theobald, in the first act of *The Snob*, learns that he is required to
disappear forever from the scene of his son's life, he uses a similar
tone: "Kein Mensch wird uns zumuten, Unbequemlichkeiten der
Übersiedlung, Schwierigkeiten neuer Wohnsitzgründung ohne
Äquivalent auf uns zu nehmen" ("No one can expect us to take
upon ourselves the inconvenience of moving, the difficulties of
finding a new home without some compensation," *R*, 158; *G*,
1:156). This is hardly a dialogue between father and son, but
rather an exchange between an employee and the company for
which he works.

It is not so much the choice of words, but rather the unusual
grammatical features which give these sentences their peculiar and
distinct flavor. Theobald's announcement "Jetzt kann ich es, dir
ein Kind zu machen, verantworten" is certainly not ungrammati-
cal. Yet the way in which the sentence separates the finite verb
"kann" from the verbal complement "verantworten" is unusual and
would be branded as ugly and stilted by any German school-
teacher. No less striking is Sternheim's tendency to express syntactical and logical connections through the position of verbs rather
than through the use of conjunctions. Theobald thus tells his wife:
"Du tust nur deine Pflicht, dankst du dem Schöpfer" ("You are
only doing your duty if you thank your Maker," *R*, 130; *G*, 1:112)
instead of "wenn du dem Schöpfer dankst." Wolke characterizes
Hicketier's unrelenting efforts to win Schippel over in the following terms: "Du kannst nicht leben, du zwängest diesen Schippel
denn" ("You cannot live, unless you can coerce this Schippel," *R*,
40; *G*, 1:493), which is a slightly archaic and highly theatrical
version of the normal sentence "Du kannst nicht leben, ausser
wenn du diessen Schippel zwingst (deinem Willen zu folgen)."
Elsbeth's critique of Krull, quoted above, would have to be "corrected" in the same way. A normal speaker might say: "Hat deine

Versicherung, *dass* Seidenschnur verzichtet, überhaupt *einen* Wert, *wenn* du sie in *einem* solchen Zustand abgibst?" Elsbeth's sentence, by contrast, separates verb and verbal complement (hat . . . Wert), it omits the conjunctions ("*dass*" and "*wenn*") as well as the articles which would be expected in a normal sentence. This omission is the third prominent feature to be mentioned here. It also occurs in such sentences as "Mein Leben steht vor vollkommener Wendung" (*G*, 1:155); "Man muss älter sein als Sie, Beziehungen von Mensch zu Mensch im Kern zu erkennen. Halten wir uns an äusserlich Sichtbares" (*G*, 1:450); "Sie hatten Schaum auf Lippen" (*G*, 1:460).[11]

Sternheim's heroes, a critic might conclude, imitate and exaggerate linguistic tendencies characteristic of bureaucratic and legal exposés, tendencies which may be acceptable on paper but which are contrary to the language of theater. The last conclusion, however, would be erroneous. Being noncolloquial, Sternheim's language requires a high degree of discipline on the part of the actors; above all, it prohibits any leisurely manner of speech. Both the separation of finite verb and verbal complement and the omission of conjunctions make one single and tensely structured unit out of sentences which otherwise would be only loosely connected. This makes it difficult, furthermore, to judge the logical coherence of these statements, a difficulty which the spectators share with the speakers' opponents and which has an unquestionable dramatic effect as well. Statements of intent are meant not to be discussed, but to be accepted and obeyed. They try to escape the grasp of critical reasoning. This is not to say that Sternheim's heroes do not reason; they do so, however, in a apodictic form, and they prefer generalized statements to observations on singular events. This may be one, and perhaps the primary, reason for the omission of articles. The sentence "Mein Leben steht vor vollkommener Wendung" is a highly dramatic statement, not an empirical description of some particular situation. In the same way, the appeal "Halten wir uns an äusserlich Sichtbares" does not refer to a specific situation. It cites a general law.

If Sternheim's nonheroes try to be impressive through the use of metaphors, his genuine heroes achieve the same effect by applying rhetorical principles developed in legal debates and by using a quasi-philosophical manner of argumentation which interprets the banalities and ambiguities of daily life in the light of some universal and immutable law. The hero is at his strongest when he can pose as the original source of the law. This is Elsbeth's case:

Ohne das Gefühl: meine einzige Verwandte ist das Weib eines Mannes, der seinen unwandelbaren Willen an der richtigen Stelle durchsetzt, wäre meine Absichten um mein Erbe der Boden entzogen.

If I didn't feel that the husband of my sole relative were a man who could make his unalterable will prevail in the right places, my intentions in regard to my estate might become irrelevant. (*S*, 102; *G*, 1:379)

He is almost as strong, however, if he can claim an expert knowledge of the law as Theobald does throughout *The Bloomers*:

THEOBALD: Könnte ich dir doch begreiflich machen, jedes Ärgernis der Welt stammt aus dem Nichtzusammengehen zweier ein Ding bildenden Faktoren.
LUISE: Hör auf; ich ertrage es nicht länger.
THEOBALD (laut): Zweier ein Ding bildenden Faktoren! Mein Amt, dein Aussehen gehen nicht zusammen.

THEOBALD: If I could only make you grasp the fact that all the trouble in the world arises when two factors forming one entity are incongruous.
LOUISE: Stop, I can't bear it any longer.
THEOBALD: (loudly) Two factors forming one entity. (*R*, 81; *G*, 1:30)

The culprit, who does not know the law, cannot possibly contradict the expert. He can only hope for his silence.

To develop an adequate stage language was one of the major concerns of early twentieth-century playwrights. The naturalistic efforts to eliminate the difference between theater and life by giving a quasi-phonological reproduction of everyday language had met with the aesthetic opposition of the literary schools which followed. The *fin-de-siècle* dramatists and the proponents of an "intimate theater" had tried to reaesthetize drama by creating lyrical situations and by using the language of poetry. On the other hand, there were attempts to rediscover earlier cultic and religious forms of theater. Such attempts were generally characterized by a sublime disregard for modern social reality. To a certain extent or—to be more precise—within the limitations of the comic genre, Sternheim's use of language presents a viable alternative to the pitfalls of both naturalism and *l'art pour l'art* theater. Without exception, the figures of his plays speak a language which conforms to the requirements of the stage, and all their statements are well integrated into the dramatic structure of the plays. Yet, at the same time, this language is strikingly "realistic" and certainly allows the expression of the concerns of everyday middle-class life.

The Social Function of Comedy

The opposition against the increasingly abstract nature of human perception is one of the primary motivations in the development of both vitalism and turn-of-the-century aestheticism. In this opposition the comic playwright is still in complete agreement with the collector and the dandy, and his creation, the comic hero, is the true cousin of the "great personalities" which the young aesthete Sternheim had looked for in history and which he had wished to present in his tragedies. In Sternheim's version, both the tragic and the comic hero are possessed by their "innermost truth" and remain true to themselves regardless of the "occurrences of the world" and regardless of the comments which others make about them.

Both heroic tragedy and farcical comedy also belong to the same age of literary history and to the same literary system. Young Sternheim's version of the tragic hero has its literary antecedent in the passionate figures of seventeenth-century classical tragedy, and his own play *Don Juan* exhibits important characteristics of representational forms of art as they were developed in courtly society, and as they survived, above all, in nineteenth-century opera. The same is true for Sternheim's comedies. In various forms, they all follow the model of Molière's plays, and the extent to which Sternheim is indebted to the seventeenth-century French playwright can hardly be overestimated. He seems to have regarded him as his immediate predecessor and alter ego, and whenever he discusses Molière, he quite naturally comments on his own plays, thus presenting at least fragments of his own theory of comedy.

How can one explain, Sternheim asks in an essay published in 1912,[12] that Molière can still serve as a model for a twentieth-century writer. The answer which he gives points at some basic social similarities between the ages of Louis XIV and of Wilhelm II. The two historical periods, Sternheim argues, witnessed both the ascent of the bourgeoisie and its decline as a coherent social class. The bourgeois were strong enough only as long as they restricted their activities to the realm of economics. As soon as they had gained sufficient financial power, they started venturing out of their proper domains and, above all, they started squandering their energies and their resources by attempting to meet the aristocracy in a decidedly nonbourgeois field: in mannerisms, in public appearance, in the pursuit of cultural values. It is within this historical situation, the essay continues, that Molière's—and thus Sternheim's—comedies acquired their specific social function. Molière, Sternheim says, wrote his plays with the intention of helping the middle classes rediscover their true character. Above all, his plays exposed to the public the syndrome of the *bourgeois gentilhomme*, of the social climber who loses both his money and his dignity in trying to imitate the aristocrats. Molière, therefore, assigned to himself the task of making the members of his own social class aware of their wrong drives and foul aspirations, and of conveying to them the message: "Bourgeois, remain true to yourself" (*G*, 6:16)[13]

The play which seems to have impressed Sternheim most of all in this respect is Molière's comedy *George Dandin*. It shows the sad fate of a wealthy bourgeois who has married an impoverished nobleman's daughter. In the course of the play, he is not only openly cuckolded by his wife, but also ridiculed by his in-laws. Unlike other would-be social climbers who are presented in Molière's comedies, however, George Dandin is, according to Sternheim, already a positive figure. At least he recognizes the mechanisms which have led to his defeat. He is not yet capable, however, of devising a successful strategy which would help him out of his dilemma. Only in *The Misanthrope*, Sternheim concludes, did Molière show a totally positive hero. The play's central figure, Alceste, is possessed by the drive to start a new life of his own "far away from the all too many all too equal" (*G*, 6:17).

Sternheim has, in later interpretations of his own plays, described the Maskes and Schippel in similar terms. Yet, whereas Alceste's example may be central to the construction of Sternheim's later comedy *Tabula Rasa*, it is unlikely that this model was already essential for the comedies discussed do far. They can, however, be read as answers to George Dandin's predicament. The first potential answer is given by Theobald Maske, who refrains from pursuing any goals which lie outside his realm. The principle which guides his actions, "Cobbler stick to your last," is the exact replica of the message which Sternheim ascribes to Molière's works. The second strategy is apparently devised for the benefit of those who feel the urge to pursue George Dandin's path. Schippel and Christian Maske venture into realms higher than their own, and their success follows from a game of good conmanship. If the higher classes try to use their cultural domains as instruments of power, a cunning comic hero can easily use the same cultural forms for his own purposes. He can outplay those above him in their own realm, the stage.

Sternheim's plays, to summarize these observations, interpret Wilhelminian society as if it were a belated *ancien régime*, that is, as a society characterized by a competitive struggle between the aristocracy and the middle classes and, at the same time, by a power structure which can be described in theatrical terms.[14] Within this interpretation, political and aesthetic impulses are allowed to converge. By advising the middle classes to remain "true to themselves" and to disregard the cultural displays of the aristocracy, the playwright Sternheim could cast himself in the role of a class-conscious author,[15] and he could do so without giving up his aesthetic beliefs. As he had done in earlier years, he still sides with the aristocrats who master the art of self-representation. He also admires, again on aesthetic grounds, those truly bourgeois characters whose actions clearly follow the law of profitability; he can

also admire, finally, the bourgeois con man who manages to out-
smart the aristocrats on their own ground. His wrath, however, is
aroused by those members of the middle class who have been
blinded by aesthetics and ideologies. In his view, they are not only
unsuccessful in their own lives, but, being "the bad copies of already flawed models," they fail to contribute to the aesthetic qualities of social life. They "enact their own silence" and are to be
considered nonentities on society's theater.

In a second Molière essay, Sternheim again combines these
two—aesthetic and political—sides of his program.[16] Written in
1917, the essay is concerned less with Molière than with a problem
of great political relevance. Sternheim's central question is, how
did the German government succeed in turning the people into
supporters of the war? In his answer he points at a superstructure
of cultural beliefs, aesthetic ideals, and ideological tenets, which,
according to Sternheim, has its culminating point in heroic tragedy.[17] The seventeenth-century middle class, he argues in a clear
attempt to circumvent the suspicions of Wilhelminian censors, was
the victim of heavy ideological brainwashing. Presented with an
heroic image of itself through the medium of the *tragédie
classique*—read, "German war propaganda"—it had started con-
sidering itself a quasi-heroic being. The middle class could thus be
turned into the useful, and even enthusiastic, pawn of the Sun
King's expansionist policies. Molière—read, "Sternheim"—who
recognized the political goals to which these heroic images were
put, tried to use his own comedies as a counterbalance. He
portrayed the members of the middle class as ordinary selfish human beings, thus trying to impress on them the fact that it was
not their natural destiny to excel on the fields of patriotic glory.

Comedy as the antidote to poisonous political propaganda! In
pursuing this goal, the comic genre also serves socio-aesthetic purposes. Theater, Sternheim argues, has the task of keeping all of
man's qualities "polished and shining" (*G*, 6:31). Above all it is to
counterbalance the tendency of society to repress certain human
characteristics in favor of others. A playwright must pay special attention to such "moribund" human traits;[18] he must try to keep
them alive; and he can achieve this goal most effectively by pre-

senting the public with dramatic figures who are totally and even excessively obsessed by them.

The history of Sternheim criticism, as well as the stage history of his plays, clearly show that the author's audience was not willing to accept the interpretational framework which has just been sketched. Sternheim's critics saw no reason to sympathize with the heroes of his plays, to share their joy, or to appreciate the author's attempts to keep alive the "sometimes brutal tinge" of the bourgeois character. With only a few exceptions, they have regarded these plays as satirical denunciations of the worst elements of bourgeois society.[19]

The critics did notice, of course, that Sternheim's works diverged from the classical form of satire. The author does not explicitly judge his dramatic figures in the light of any ideals, nor does he introduce into his plays any reliable commentators. Sternheim's comedies, the critics observed, know only cynics and fools, power-hungry winners and deluded losers; they completely instrumentalize anything that might be called a value, and they turn sisters, mothers, and fathers into objects of trade, just as they ridicule love and affection. In this manner, however, they were thought to give a very accurate picture of the disastrous turn which bourgeois society had taken in the course of the twentieth century. On the one hand, the critics concluded, Sternheim's plays mirror the unrestrained drives which determine the real actions of the middle classes; on the other hand, by portraying idealists as fools, they expose the uses to which twentieth-century society has put the once venerable ideals which the middle class had developed in its period of ascent.

Such interpretations have determined the overall reception of Sternheim's comedies and, compared with this rather stringent line, the interpretative changes which can be observed were only of minor importance. Before World War I, most critics interpreted Sternheim's works more as satires on specific and limited segments of social life. After the collapse of the Wilhelminian regime, the author was praised for having uncovered the rottenness of society at large and for having anticipated and even contributed to its breakdown. After World War II, finally, some critics were even able to discern in Sternheim's plays forebodings of the Nazi period. The petty bourgeois Theobald Maske, they argued, was the very type of person who, a few decades later, would have joined Hitler's storm troopers.[20]

It is by now widely acknowledged that such satirical readings of the texts contradict the author's original intentions. Yet, many critics argue that a satirical interpretation is justified insofar as it comes closer to the objective meaning of the comedies than the interpretations which Sternheim himself had suggested. In trying to present his real-to-life bourgeois heroes as model figures, Sternheim simply misjudged the social reality of his time or, as the East German critic Hans Kaufmann put it: "The theorist Sternheim overlooks 'only' one fact, a fact which the dramatist had worked out very clearly and which constitutes the wit of his comedies: the individual and true character of the Maskes, deprived of its ideological surface appearance, is nothing but the perfect bourgeois character. The 'truly personal' is the socially typical without a halo."[21]

The younger Sternheim's oppositional aestheticism, as was pointed out earlier, bears close resemblance to Wilhelminian aesthetics and, similarly, his attempts to present unchained drives as expressions of an individual's "own incomparable desires" leads to the paradoxical result that supposedly individual and truly personal characteristics coincided with that which is psychologically the most common. Hans Kaufmann's interpretation sees the same mechanism at work in Sternheim's comedies.

However, against this interpretation it must be pointed out that it was not necessarily Sternheim's original intention to present in his comedies that which might be called a "truly personal character."[22] The Molière essay ascribes this quality to the *Misanthrope* only. Both the Maskes and Schippel, on the other hand, are quite clearly fashioned after the model of George Dandin; they are conceived as representatives of their social class. They are thus meant to represent the "perfect bourgeois character . . . without a halo."

And yet it cannot be denied that a certain amount of uneasiness remains in the face of these plays. If one admits that it was Sternheim's intention to encourage the middle classes to remain true to their "bourgeois character," one would still have to ask on what grounds such encouragement could be justified under the conditions of twentieth-century society. Wilhelminian society, to be sure, retained feudal relics, and its stability depended to a great extent on the use of ideologies and images, many of which had been carried over from an earlier historical period. On the other hand, the essential positions of power were already in the hands of the bourgeois and the social system of the period was already thoroughly capitalistic. The ideological relics were thus no longer instruments of power used by the aristocracy; many of them had already shifted into the hands of the bourgeois themselves.

Seen within this framework, that which had been meant as the enjoyable triumph of the social underdog turns into the macabre victory of the bourgeois master who has found an additional instrument to enslave those who are already in his power. With the exception of Schippel, none of the heroes portrayed in Sternheim's comedies has to fight a truly uphill battle. Theobald not only prevails over Scarron, who is socially superior to him, he also triumphs over Luise who, from beginning to end, is the loser of the games which are played around her. Christian's victory over the Palens is equally ambivalent. If *The Snob* is fashioned after *George Dandin*, Sternheim may indeed be said to have misread the social realities of his time. The Palens of the twentieth century were hardly in a position to laugh at the Maskes;[23] it is quite as likely that the Maskes had already started to laugh at them, and it is certain that they had already donned the masks of quasi-feudal sovereigns in order to give their economic power an additional base of support.[24] In *The Strongbox*, finally, the theatrical games are described as middle-class infights from beginning to end, and it becomes clear here that this whole concept of dramatization cannot break out of the vicious dialectics of the master-slave relationship. If Krull frees himself by assuming the position of director, he still needs someone else who is willing to play the part of the comic fool and to be the "bad copy of an already flawed model."

Sternheim's plays—thus the conclusion to which such observations lead—function as nonsatirical comedies only under two conditions. A reader must either accept the premise that Wilhelminian society was still basically an *ancien regime* in which the middle classes were fighting an uphill battle, or he must be willing to agree that in the first decades of this century—or for that matter in our own time—it is, above all, the tight grip of cultural idols and repressive ideologies which prevents the average citizen from realizing his human potential. Against these particular oppressive powers a type of comedy which encourages the spectator to shed his inhibitions and to give free rein to his drives may indeed be an appropriate remedy. Unfortunately, however, Sternheim's plays depict more than the blissful existence of the middle-class hedonist. They also show that no master can do without his slaves and that the cunning middle-class pragmatist is victorious only if he can firmly count on the folly of others. In this respect, Sternheim's comedies are certainly realistic, but the more a reader emphasizes this particular quality, the more difficulties he may have in appreciating their truly comic features.

The following chapters will show that Sternheim himself became increasingly aware of these inner contradictions of his dramatic and political tenets. In *1913*, the drama following *The Snob*, he clearly updates his picture of modern society. The play takes place within leading capitalistic circles, and its actions are no longer simply a matter of private concern. The playwright must, therefore, once again consider the general social implications of his beliefs. In doing so, Sternheim goes beyond the limits both of the comic genre and of middle-class society. According to the central thesis of the play, the existing social system has exhausted its potential. Its dealings have become counterproductive; a "new formula" has to be found. The next play, *Tabula Rasa*, ends on the same tenor. As is documented by both plays, Sternheim is trying to leave the contradictions of bourgeois society behind him. Like other contemporary writers, he is beginning to advocate a general cultural revolution.[25]

Chapter Seven

Toward an Anarchist Revolution

1913

The drama *1913*[1] was written, Sternheim noted in later years, to demonstrate "how far bourgeois affairs had, in all innocence perhaps, progressed" (*G*, 6:46). "Bourgeois affairs," of course, led to the war, and if it is true that Sternheim had originally intended to make this point, he could hardly have chosen a better title for the play. Later critics have often marveled at the author's insights and prophetic gift, and it is certainly true that Sternheim, due to his background and his upper-class connections, had acquired a better inside knowledge of the mechanisms of capitalist society than most writers of his period.[2] Yet it would be wrong to say that the relationship between economic developments on the one hand and the outbreak of the war on the other constituted the playwright's major concern or that the imminence of war is one of the play's major topics. Rather, *1913* voices a very general and yet surprisingly perspicacious critique of modern capitalism. The critique, as will be seen, is mostly based on the aestheticist beliefs which Sternheim adhered to throughout his life. At the same time, the play shows that the author was slowly moving closer to expressionist circles or that, at least, he was attentively viewing this new movement with a mixture of fascination and skepticism.[3]

There is an element of nostalgia inherent in most forms of anti-capitalist criticism. Middle-class writers who pursue this line normally present a state of society which was still sane and promising as opposed to the dark and depraved features of contemporary reality. In most instances in German literature, either the Renaissance or the age of Goethe have served this function of contrastive imagery. Sternheim, in *1913*, uses the same technique, although he chooses to work within a more limited historical framework. His point of reference is the 1870s, the period in which Germany started to develop into a heavily industrialized country; and it is thus an earlier and a later period of industrialization which he contrasts.

Translated into dramatic form, this contrast is presented as the antagonism of different generations within a capitalistic dynasty, the house of Maske. Christian, the hero of the previous play, is by now seventy years old and one of the most influential and powerful industrialists. He is, at the same time, the representative of a better past, especially when compared to his children Philipp Ernst and Sofie, who are the embodiments of modern depravity. Further participants in the dramatic action are two young intellectuals of whom one, Friedrich Stadler, bears some vague likeness to Ernst Stadler, an early expressionist poet whom Sternheim befriended in these years. The other one, Christian's secretary Wilhelm Krey, writes anticapitalist pamphlets and is a leader of one of the factions of the German youth movement.

Of Christian's children, Philipp Ernst, the oldest, serves mainly as comic relief in an otherwise tense and somewhat abstract atmosphere. He is an imbecile dandy whose major concern is keeping up with the latest fads in men's clothing. He gets a headache whenever he hears a simple business term and is overjoyed to trade his share of the family's power for a dandy's gag—a watch chain of simple string attached to two platinum fasteners and worn on a dress coat. His formula for life is comfort. "I never, under any circumstances, expose myself to attacks on my peace of mind" (*R*, 211; *G*, 1:239); he dreads any "untoward accidents" since "they are always embarrassing intervals between two pleasant events" (*R*, 208; *G*, 1:235); and if war should break out he intends to retire to some fashionable spa or embark upon a trip around the world.

If this "average heir" (*R*, 212; *G*, 1:241) typifies the upper-class degenerate of the second generation, a phenomenon often described by biographers of capitalist families, his sister Sofie represents the threatening aspects of modern capitalist leadership. Germany, Christian explains early in the play, is a country where

"65 million people are crammed on 500 thousand square miles." Such overcrowding leads to the hypertrophic development of two drives: "the belly hunger of the plebs, and the power hunger of the rich" (*R*, 205; *G*, 1:230). Sofie is an embodiment of this second drive. She is the perfect example "of a modern human being motivated solely by the lust for power" (*R*, 205; *G*, 1:229), and it is made clear during the play that her success will, in this respect, surpass that of her father.

Christian is a basically conservative character who thinks that boom and depression periods should follow each other like summer and winter,[4] and who favors an organic growth of society. Sofie has replaced such concepts by her sole interest in expansion, and the means which she has at her disposal are much more highly developed than those which her father had been able to use. Masses of petty stockholders have provided Sofie with money and hence with an amount of power which by far surpasses her own financial means: "It's not the few millions one possesses oneself, it's the enormous sums which the public entrusts to a handful of men and which they can use at will that gives them their incomparable power" (*R*, 212: *G*, 1:242).

The fact that the new type of capitalist works within anonymous institutions and with borrowed money also means that he can shed the princely and individualistic qualities which had been characteristic of the older generation. In pursuing her goals, Sofie Maske does not risk losing anything; she cannot be made privately or publicly accountable for her actions. Christian Maske was still a public person and, as such, he had to be concerned if not about his morals, then at least about his reputation. Sofie, on the other hand, works from a position of complete anonymity. The glory, if there is any, will be her husband's. She herself will never be known to the public. She is thus comparable to a spider who has woven an invisible web and is waiting for her prey to get strangled (*R*, 202; *G*, 1:226). And there is no way that this prey can escape her. Either as money lenders or as consumers, the public will fall into her web. New techniques have been developed to deprive middle-class consumers even of their ability to form wishes of their own. Sofie "knows every customer like the back of her hand, knows what his instincts will automatically tell him to do and keeps firing instructions which he takes for his own wishes" (*R*, 203; *G*, 1:223). Capitalist society has thus turned into an Orwellian nightmare. It is a society where a few anonymous figures are omnipotent and where the rest of the population have completely abdicated their willpower.

The critique of capitalism voiced here takes up notions which Sternheim already hinted at in earlier plays, especially in *Don Juan*, where a society in which the masses wish to be bled in the service of a great leader is mentioned.[5] Sternheim now systematizes these elements and transfers them from the political to the economic sphere: the loss of human individualism and freedom is the result of the capitalistic concentration of economic power and of the emergence of a modern consumer society. In this society even the concept of individualism has no chance to survive. Increasingly surrounded by throw-away goods, man learns to consider himself a cheap product which can be discarded as fast as it is produced: "the mass consumption of all the goods in his daily life has brainwashed him till he is unaware of any individual value and consumes and discards feelings, judgments, and even himself and is incapable of imparting any quality to them" (*R*, 237; *G*, 1:284).

Interestingly enough, it is mainly Christian Maske, the representative of the older generation of capitalists, who voices this very precise critique. He has the inside knowledge of the system which he helped create and which he has seen develop. Compared to his analyses, the anticapitalistic statements of Krey, the representative of the young generation, remain on the level of flowery generalities. Krey expresses a political philosophy which is characterized by anti-Western nationalism, romantic anticapitalism, and a back-to-nature religion, a blend which was quite typical of the German youth movement of the time.

The Germans, Krey believes, are a nation representing specific virtues; they have, however, so far neglected to develop their true character. Above all, they have been led into temptation by "the international rush for gold" (*R*, 198; *G*, 1:220). In order to rediscover their original character, they should stop looking across national borders and concentrate on themselves. "While it is true,"

Krey says, that "we desire to be humane beings, above all we wish to be Germans" (*R*, 198; *G*, 1:220). To achieve this goal, a struggle against the "speculations of international finance" (*R*, 215; *G*, 1:272) has to be started: "we should aim at real values instead of the production of trash" (*R*, 232; *G*, 1:272).

According to Stadler, Krey is leading the young people back from "the fever clouds of stock market hysteria to the crystal-streams of our forests" (*R*, 216; *G*, 1:247). The young generation sees in his ideas a new hope for a "national future which had more than mere human appeal; it appealed to us as men." His words "forced youth up on its feet, ready to march shoulder to shoulder" with him (*R*, 215; *G*, 1:246).

For later critics, Krey has been an embodiment of the conservative side of the German youth movement. His blend of nationalism, the cult of leadership, and irrational anticapitalism, it has been said, is one of the ideological amalgamates which the National Socialists later incorporated into their thinking. Within the play, Krey is given a highly ambivalent, if not ironic, treatment. For Sofie, he is a "loafer" whose "Platonic drivel" is both harmless and boring (*R*, 237; *G*, 1:283). Stadler, on the other hand, considers him the new Messiah, and Christian hopes that Krey might become the Mirabeau of modern times and prepare a social upheaval equal to the French Revolution.

To do justice to such hopes, Krey would, however, have to meet two conditions. He has to find the "right formula" for a reorganization of society, and he needs a "pure heart" (*R*, 240; *G*, 1:287). As it turns out, Krey is a failure on both accounts. Most of his critical thoughts bear the stigma of lower-middle-class sentimentality and, just as importantly, the new leader Krey cannot escape the dialectics of the former slave turned master. Krey has a taste for personal power and a penchant for the delights which wealth can bestow. Both are sufficient to corrupt his purity of mind. His last appearance on stage shows him in front of the mirror trying on Philipp Ernst's new clothes. He is not a new Mirabeau, but at best another social climber.

This leaves Christian Maske as the only one who can voice a serious critique of capitalist society. Yet his statements retain a high degree of ambivalence as well. On what grounds, Sofie asks, can her actions be criticized by her own father? The differences between her business and his maneuvers, she points out, are not substantive but only technical ones. She is following older principles of action and working within a system which she has inherited and for whose creation she is not responsible. If she can operate on a vastly expanded scale and with greater success than her predecessors, this is only due to technical improvements and perhaps to her greater skill. Christian's objections, she remarks, smack of sentimentality, and he can hardly attack her without denying his own character and past.

Such arguments are more than a mere dramatic rebuttal. They point to a dilemma in which the author of *1913* found himself while writing the play. On what grounds, one can indeed ask, could Sternheim himself criticize the type of modern capitalist represented by Sofie Maske? Had he not in his previous plays encouraged the bourgeoisie to remain true to its character, had he not presented such figures as Theobald and Christian Maske as model heroes, and are Sofie's actions more than a necessary result of that which Sternheim had praised before?

To return to the level of the play, Christian Maske does indeed show that he is incapable of objecting to Sofie's character. She exemplifies the hypertrophic development of a human drive, the lust for power. As an embodiment of this drive she is, however, still a striking personality and, for Christian, less an object of horror than of admiration. Her business dealings, he says, clearly bear the sign of genius (*R*, 207; *G*, 1:233). Krey tries to object that this evaluation is valid only "on the assumption that life on earth consists entirely in the acquisition of material goods" (*R*, 207; *G*, 1:233). This objection, however, is quickly brushed aside: "The rest, old fellow-me-lad, you can keep to yourself. Or do you want to show moral indignation, cough up relics of your childhood education?" (*R*, 207; *G*, 1:233).

This short rebuttal is characteristic both of Sternheim's critique of capitalism and of his attitude toward those younger writers who tried to criticize society by reverting to the tenets of petty bourgeois sentimentality.[6] Both Sternheim and Christian Maske are un-willing to admit that "the acquisition of material goods" is not a high goal in life nor are they prepared to give up their particular brand of aestheticism, their admiration for "great personalities." Christian Maske thus cannot help admiring his daughter Sofie; and yet he tries to use the same aesthetic criteria to denounce the economic system within which she excels. In his view, modern capitalism has disastrous effects on the overall aesthetic quality of life. The founding fathers, who belonged to the generation of Christian Maske, had still been "public persons" "visible" to oth-ers. They had been willing not only to gather the profits, but also to accept the risks inherent in their business transactions and, finally, they had not blindly promoted the principles of standardi-zation and of mass production. "I've told you time and again," Christian says to Sofie, "in addition to your frantic pursuit of methods for doubling and trebling the production of certain arti-cles you should also have all factories and laboratories work on means to improve their quality" (*R*, 238; *G*, 1:284). Sofie's re-sponse that she has never heard her father express such thoughts before may be an expression of Sternheim's own doubts in the face of the contrast which he builds up here between the aesthetically oriented earlier capitalists and their power-hungry heirs.

For the play itself, however, and for Sternheim's attempt to combine his hymn on the individual early bourgeois with a cri-tique of the capitalist system, this contrast is essential. Above all, it allows Sternheim to portray his spokesman Christian as the prin-cipal advocate of a revolutionary turnover. Christian Maske, to be sure, is not assigned the role of a prophet; he functions, however, as the prophet's mentor and judge, and he will—as he says—also be his first disciple once the right formula is found. "Do your best," he exhorts Krey, "light the fuse under the powder-keg. If a new régime arises I'm ready to start from scratch. Corporal or General—as long as I'm right in the thick of it" (*R*, 219; *G*, 1:252).

Life for Christian has always been a battle field or a racing ground. He always drove in the highest gear (*R*, 201; *G*, 1:224), and he still "bursts through the house like a bomb"; when he is "in the room it's as if the door's been left open" (*R*, 201; *G*, 1:22), and even at the age of seventy his battle with Sofie is a source of pleasure for him. He is still like a "flame" (*R*, 208; *G*, 1:234), and he will once more open "the flood gate of ideas" and "sweep aside" his daughter.

In *1913*, more than in his earlier plays, Sternheim develops a system of metaphors in which things and persons are seen as explosives, as batteries, as machines in high motion, or as atavistic beasts in exotic jungles. Besides Christian, there is Sofie, who is said to think "in explosive discharges" (*R*, 202; *G*, 1:226). Ottilie, Christian's third child, is told that she should let "claws grow" and depart for life, for she has "got her wings" (*R*, 237; *G*, 1:228). This too is the attractive side of Krey. The "fire of his resolution is inspiring his peers" (*R*, 215; *G*, 1:246), and his words have "fanned the embers to flames" (*R*, 214; *G*, 1:245).

This metaphorical system, obviously indebted to vitalist philosophy, remains an important ingredient of Sternheim's thinking. History, according to these concepts, is composed of explosive and creative periods on the one hand, and of static and dull periods on the other. The capitalism of the founding fathers had attractive elements: they brought about a new and fascinating era and produced great personalities. Now, however, this historical period has exhausted its aesthetic and vital potential, and it is, according to Sternheim's thinking, time for society to become productive again and to add a new set of statues to the museum of history.

It is for this reason above all that both Christian Maske and the author Sternheim opt for change and advocate a cultural revolution which will once again make life fascinating. It is for this reason too that from 1914 on Sternheim breaks with the figures of the cultural establishment and drifts into the circles of radicalism and—after the war—tries to present himself as the prophet of a new era. The end of the drama *1913* is the first example of this new tendency. Christian Maske is dead, his children and Wilhelm Krey are hopelessly corrupt. Friedrich Stadler remains and is presented in a closing scene full of hollow pathos.[7] He must leave the house of the capitalists and will have to find his way through the night:

BUTLER: A light perhaps?
FRIEDRICH: A light must be found. God willing—a light toward the
great goal. (Exits through the door center.)
(Butler turns off all the lights, opens the window. The wind blows the
curtains into the room.) (*R*, 244; *G*, 1:294)

Tabula Rasa

Cicero has been killed, the *pater patriae* is dead, the republic is
in danger—so goes the scenario of an early eighteenth-century German tragicomedy.[8] Enter Harlequin. He grabs Cicero's head, puts
it into a bag, and hurries off to Cicero's daughter. His interest in
the historical occurrence is the tip which he can expect as a carrier
boy.

Sternheim's play *Tabula Rasa*[9] is certainly less drastic in its use
of farcical elements, yet it follows the same basic structures. On an
elevated level, it is a political drama and the issues discussed are of
considerable importance. The scene is a factory town on the occasion of a company's fiftieth anniversary. It is time to think not
only about the future of one business enterprise, but also about the
future of society at large.

Sternheim presents this part of the action in the form of a
dispute between two leftist politicians. One of them, the moderate
Social Democrat Artur Flocke, fights for the establishment of a society which knows only equal citizens. His political strategy reads
like this:

Conquest of the political power through the proletariat and its party organization. . . . But not in a violent form, but through peaceful evolution. The privileged citizen will be replaced by the equality of all members of society. The Social Democrats do not dissolve the existing society
and they do not make proletarians out of its members, but they raise the
worker from the level of proletarianism to that of the bourgeois, and they
universalize the bourgeois status." (*G*, 2:188)

Flocke's short-range goal is to improve the workers' cultural opportunities. It is his demand that the company, in honor of its
fiftieth anniversary, build a library and present it as a gift to its
workers. Flocke's opponent Sturm abhors such moderate evolution-

ary strategies. He is a political radical, and for him the ongoing
festivities are a good occasion to fan the sparks of the workers'
petty dissatisfaction into the burning flames of the revolution.
The proletariat, according to him, will have to "seize the political
power," it will have "to abolish all class distinctions," and it will
reach these goals only "through bloody violence" (*G*, 2:245). The
construction of a library would, from this point of view, only help
the bourgeoisie in their attempts to corrupt the minds of the proletarians. For Sturm, the cultural as well as the technical offerings of
capitalism are nothing but allurements used by those in power to
divert the workers from their true interests.

In political terms, the subject of the play is the infight between
ultraradical and moderate leftist factions, an infight which has
haunted the European leftist movements since the days of the
French Revolution. There is, however, a third party to this struggle. His name is Ständer; he is a sixty-year-old blue-collar worker
and, in the true fashion of Harlequin, he manages to turn this dramatic political confrontation into a farce. Not only does he change
the nature of the game, he directs it, calls the actors together,
prompts them, introduces them, and dismisses them as soon as the
game is over, that is, as soon as his interests have been met.

Not unlike Theobald Maske, Ständer has one major goal in life:
to reach the age of retirement in full possession of his physical and
mental health and with control over sufficient financial means. At
the beginning of the play he seems close to reaching this goal. He
has neither wife nor children—both would be sources of expense
and worry—but only a housekeeper named Bertha who works for
almost nothing. Her occasional demands for a higher salary are cut
short by a set of arguments familiar in all societies characterized by
the exploitation of labor and a facade of freedom. Bertha's salary,
Ständer tells her, cannot be raised since their relationship is not
based on contracts, but on mutual understanding. After all,
Ständer is not a capitalistic exploiter, and Bertha is beyond the historical stage of alienation. She works only to develop to the fullest
her own individual potential. What a marvellous experience to
clean up the pigsty! Why doesn't she do it first thing next morning? (*G*, 2:166).

This exploitative attitude is typical of all of Ständer's actions. He knows that for a man who wants to keep body and soul together the moment's pleasures are not to be sacrificed for later goods. Act 1 shows him, secretly of course, feasting on rare delicacies while his niece Isolde displays her female charms to him by posing as an allegorical figure. He keeps her in his house solely for such purposes. His days in the factory are equally pleasurable to the senses. Ständer's salary is much higher than that of a normal worker since he is a skilled glass blower. He has thus been able to buy a moderate amount of the company's shares. Since the work in the factory is mechanized, however, there is no work left for skilled workers, and Ständer and his colleague Heinrich Flocke can thus make full use of the modern sanitary equipment which the management has installed for its employees. They spend most of their working hours under the hot showers or in the bath tubs.

This privileged position is—and here the plot line starts—endangered by the forthcoming anniversary of the factory. Ständer is afraid of a general cleanup which might lead to the discovery of his dronelike position. He tries to avert this danger by creating an atmosphere of general unrest which is to last until the festivities are over and normal work can resume. Hence the demand for a library, which had been his idea; hence too, since the management seems all too willing to give in, a telegram which Ständer sends the radical Sturm, asking him to stir things up still more. Not too much, of course, since Ständer also has to consider his interests as a stockholder and a future recipient of retirement benefits. Ständer, therefore, sends a second telegram, this time to call onto the scene the moderate Flocke, who is assigned the task of calming down the emotions which the other political actor has been able to arouse.

Ständer knows that he will succeed as long as he can keep these two forces in balance and still create the appearance of general commotion. He must be careful, however, and make sure that neither of his two actors succeeds in winning over the public completely. Thus he accompanies them on their public appearances; he tries to prompt them and to counterbalance their words whenever necessary:

STURM: Whenever I sow one kind of seed, if I turn away and turn back again, it seems to me that another kind grows. When you repeat my words to the people, you wink so ambivalently that they are bound to misunderstand.

STÄNDER: I do?

STURM: You roll your eyes, squint and speak out of the corner of your mouth. You are like an overwrought signal on green for go acting as if it were on red for stop. (*G*, 2:203)

With this strategy everything runs smoothly for Ständer. Events take only one dangerous turn—when the management, in order to document its solidarity with the workers, offers Ständer the position of co-director. To accept it would, of course, be catastrophic for Ständer's health. He proposes old Flocke instead, who promptly dies after a few months in office. In the meantime, Ständer has gained an early retirement with full benefits.

What does Harlequin do when the game is over? The conventional ending has him anticipate the pleasures which are in store for him and his bride. Sternheim goes even a step further. Ständer has no pleasures to anticipate since he has enjoyed them all along. He has, however, had to enjoy them in secret. Now the time of hiding is over. Doors are opened, curtains are pulled aside, and one of the last scenes shows Ständer feasting on his delicacies and contemplating his niece's charm in full view of the public. He has achieved all his goals, is independent, and thus need no longer conceal his character. Nor is there any need for him to tolerate those around him. Bertha is summarily fired. Isolde, his niece, and her bridegroom Artur Flocke enact one last loving family scene for him. Then they too are confronted with Ständer's true feelings: "Literally repulsive. From the moment I got to know you I have fought the urge to throw up at every word you say" (*G*, 2:242).

Once the comic person has gained his autonomy, he can afford to burn all the bridges. "From today on," Ständer explains, "I have free opportunities and I dissociate myself categorically from all that is propagated here as the law of man" (*G*, 2 :247). According to the outlook inherent in the play, Ständer will roam through the world searching for a new gospel of life which completely suits his character.[10]

The Utopian World of Carnival

At first sight, at least, the ending of *Tabula Rasa* adds a new and contradictory element to the preceding action. Until the closing scenes, Ständer might well be interpreted merely as a farcical figure acting within a play which bears all the characteristics of a political satire.[11] With his final statement, he suddenly gains in stature, and the author, according to the views of many critics, suddenly uses—or rather abuses—him as a spokesman for his own concept of human freedom and emancipation, disregarding the unity of Ständer's character and the unity of the play as a whole.[12]

This first impression is correct to the extent that it emphasizes the seriousness of the closing scenes. Ständer expresses many of Sternheim's thoughts. Much like his comic hero, Sternheim considered the Social Democrat reformers "repulsive" because they appeared only to give fresh support to middle-class ideologies and thus were incapable of bringing about any social change. Much like Ständer, too, Sternheim began to show a good deal of sympathy for the likes of Sturm, that is, for the radical elements of the political left. Ständer, it is true, expresses his doubts about a revolutionary strategy aimed at toppling capitalist society by violent means. The victorious revolutionaries, he thinks, would simply occupy the old positions of power and thus be prevented from bringing about any radical changes. Yet Ständer is willing to appreciate Sturm's radical impetus, and he definitely prefers him to Flocke. It will be shown below that this attitude characterizes quite well Sternheim's own relationship to leftist radicalism.

A farcical hero as the spokesman for the author and a model figure for the public: this seeming paradox can once more demonstrate the uniquely important position of theatrical concepts in Sternheim's thoughts, and it can also help to illustrate the direction in which his political and aesthetic philosophy was moving in these early war years. Theater, it was said earlier, is more than a literary medium; theatrical roles determine social interactions as well. In *Tabula Rasa*, this point is made clear once again. Ständer, very much like Theobald Maske, hides himself behind a cloak of inconspicuousness. To those around him, he appears in the mask of an honorable and politically active worker, and in this disguise he can freely follow his hedonistic drives. At the same time, he displays astounding abilities in using the roles of theater for his own purposes. His victory follows from the skill in making others play for his own benefit and pleasure.

In the earlier plays, theater—and hence society—were presented as self-contained realms. Within these limits the heroes could only attempt to reach a position at the top of the given hierarchy. The goal of their actions was power, and they could, therefore, never afford to stop playing. A director is powerless without his cast and the heroic actor is strong only as long as he stands in front of an audience. Ständer quite evidently transcends the limits of this structure. At the end of the play, he dismisses his cast. His goal is not to ensure his power, but to retain his freedom.

This does not mean, however, that Ständer abandons altogether the concepts of stagecraft. In the closing scenes, he is still a representational figure, although one acting outside of competitive social structures. His feasting behind open doors and open curtains is a demonstrative act, and it is his wish that a "newspaper or books would report on me in big print" (G, 2:240). He considers himself a figure to be emulated, and his concept of a utopian world is one in which he would be surrounded by other feasting men with whom he could share his joy and who would stimulate his pleasure. Unfortunately, he says, he is too old and has had to wait too long to serve as the leader of such a hedonistic movement. "If I were twenty . . . and did what I am doing now, many would be swept along by my rebellion. That which now only moves the prophet would then be a general prophecy" (G, 2:247).

A general departure for a paradise of hedonism: this is a recurrent utopian concept among anarchist writers. The concrete image is that of men sitting down to the full tables which they have prepared for their own joy.[13] It is within this context that both the ending of *Tabula Rasa* and Sternheim's reversal to a farcical type of comedy can best be explained. Ständer closely resembles those thoroughly sensuous characters who were the heroes of the pre-courtly and pre-middle class forms of comedy.[14] He is a cousin to the Jan Bouschets, Hans Leberwursts, Pickelherrings, and Truffaldinos whose names already indicate the appetites which govern their actions.

Within the confines of modern civilized society and its theater, these farcical heroes were generally interpreted not as stimulants of joy, but as targets of derision. At the same time, farcical comedy, the genre in which they appeared, was considered an offense to good taste and, consequently, banished from the canon of official literature. This process parallels the satirical instrumentalization of comedy which took place in the seventeenth and eighteenth centuries. On the other hand one can observe, within the tradition of middle-class aesthetics, an oppositional subcurrent of thought which, once again, gives a positive evaluation to Harlequin and his brothers on stage. Within this subcurrent, the farcical heroes as well as the precourtly forms of comedy are seen as images of freedom and sensual joy and as the last relics of a type of existence of which mankind was deprived in the course of history. On such grounds the philosopher Hegel, normally an advocate of law and order, could recommend to his students the comedies of Aristophanes. Without having read these plays, he observed, it is impossible even to imagine "the feeling of piggish delight which man can experience in life."[15]

It is not surprising, then, that among anarchist writers the early forms of comedy and their real-life counterparts, the Dionysian rites in ancient Greece and the carnivalistic tradition in sixteenth century Europe, could command a high degree of attention. These forms seemed to portray a freedom of life which could also serve as a model for future societies. Thoughts of this nature first appear in Rousseau's writings;[16] they play a prominent part in the thinking of Jean Paul, Heine, and Nietzsche, and are prominent in early twentieth-century anarchist circles. Many of the activities of the Dada movement were clearly aimed at turning life into a great carnival; in 1929 the Soviet literary historian Michail Bachtin published books on Dostoevski and Rabelais, in which he not only investigated the carnivalistic tradition, but also proposed its revival as the best means to reestablish human freedom.[17] Among present-day French philosophers similar concepts are again of central importance.

In an essay written in the early twenties, Sternheim directly refers to this carnivalistic tradition.[18] Prewar capitalism, he says
there, had one promising feature. It might have resulted in a
reestablishment of Dionysian liberty; it could have tuned the members of the middle classes into advocates of an unrestrained hedonistic form of life. Such statements read like a belated commentary
on the images presented both at the end of *Tabula Rasa* and in
"Heidenstam" and "Der Anschluss," two stories written in 1917.
In these stories, the world of freedom is presented in the grotesque
form of an insane asylum. In it, each patient is at last given the
chance to act out his own particular drives. Restraints from the
outside world are lacking as are the inner inhibitions which prevent the individual from living up to his own potential.

Much as in Ständer's vision of a community of hedonists, each
individual member of the insane asylum is an actor who displays
his character and, at the same time, a spectator who, from
watching others, derives both pleasure and the stimuli necessary
for his own performances. Carnivalistic acting, as it appears here,
knows no script, no separation of roles, and no goals lying outside
the immediate pleasure of expressing one's character. It is, for
these reasons, the truly utopian variant of the *theatrum mundi* concept and perhaps the most appealing version of human freedom to
be found in Sternheim's works.

Chapter Eight

Sternheim's Novellas: The World as an Energy System

In Sternheim's plays, society is presented as a theater; pleasures, triumphs, and misfortunes depend on the manner in which a person enacts his own life. In the novellas which Sternheim wrote during World War I, this concept still exists; it is, however, reduced to secondary importance. Instead, the world presented here takes on the appearance of a huge power plant to which man is, in various ways, connected. His pleasures and anxieties are created by the flux and reflux of energy, by its loss and its generation, its adequate and inadequate consumption. The lives of Sternheim's fictitious characters either resemble a candle burning on an insufficient amount of wax or exist as a series of explosions. Such explosions can appear in the spasms of child birth, in yelling and screaming, in uninhibited gesticulations, in murder and love-making, and in the paroxysms of death. Social developments are described in a similar way. They can be dull and unexciting or they can erupt in warfare and revolutions. On the one hand, there is the quiet life in provincial towns, on the other, there is rush hour traffic, neon-lit streets, department stores, and the hectic pictures of silent movies, which all appear as overwhelming outbursts of social energy. Individuals either cut themselves off from the sources of vital energy by repressing their best experiences and wishes and by giving in to a life of mere routine or, if they are fortunate, they have access to an unlimited number of batteries and generators. Energy is stored in bank accounts, and money is one of its primary social manifestations; it is also stored in human skills and in works of art, which are an inexhaustible source of pleasure. It is accumulated furthermore in pregnant women, in young girls' breasts, in erect penises, in long hair, or in ripe fruits. A prostitute squanders her energy, a nun saves hers for God; a policeman who pays attention only to those who look suspicious is a wise investor of his vital resources, but he has a chilling effect on his surroundings; a lively child, by contrast, animates those around him through his exuberant vitality.

The above examples give only a small indication of the variety of energy metaphors which actually occur in Sternheim's novellas. Taken together, they result in a *vision du monde*;[1] they permit the author to give a surprisingly coherent presentation of the social life of his times. This coherence is, to be sure, somewhat obscured by the fact that each of Sternheim's novellas seems to do no more than relate the biographical development of one particular hero and consequently appears as a separate and autonomous entity. A reader who is willing to consider the whole corpus of Sternheim's prose will soon find out, however, that this appearance of autonomy is misleading. All the biographies which Sternheim presents relate not only to the same metaphorical, but also to the same structural and thematic, system. They delineate not so much individual lives, but rather recurring modes of existence whose common feature is the economics of energy. The typical hero of Sternheim's stories is thus one who sees his initial fund of vital power trickle away in the course of his life. Facing "bankruptcy," he goes through a crisis and begins to redefine his social attitudes. He may, at this point, either turn into an exploiter of others or, in other cases, form a symbiotic relationship with his fellow human beings which is characterized by a give and take of pleasure and energy and which transforms the world into a *perpetuum mobile*. It is at this point, above all, that Sternheim's prose transcends the level of merely personalized narration and becomes a utopian projection, an attempt to describe a vitalistic and aestheticist paradise.

The Decay of Life and the Birth of Exploitation

Money, as has already been said, is one of the forms in which energy manifests itself in society. To the eyes of a person living on annuities, a bank account closely resembles a self-charging battery; it seems to provide interest automatically and without the requirement of work. A good number of Sternheim's heroes—like the author himself—are in the fortunate position of having access to such an energy source. Heidenstam draws 42,000 marks in yearly dividends; Yvette is a superrich heiress; the sisters Storck inherited 180,000 marks at their father's death. Others, like the composer Schuhlin, the servant girl Meta, or the high-class prostitute Stefanie, are deprived of such riches.[2] They come from proletarian backgrounds, and Stefanie's parents, for instance, "were so poor that they roused the amazement of the shabby population in that destitute area" (*G*, 4:315).

These and similar statements, which invariably stand at the very beginning of Sternheim's novellas, are not, as might be assumed, intended to draw attention to social inequities. On the contrary, the upper-class narrator Sternheim perceives milieu and financial status as part of an individual's nature. Where bank accounts are lacking, some other source of energy can thus take their place. Schuhlin, for instance, is compensated for his lack of money through his musical talents. He accumulates musical scores in the same way as others accumulate money, and his mind resembles a "piggy bank" which he slowly fills with the products of his inspiration (*G*, 4:61). Meta, the servant girl, finds a similar substitute for her lack of money in her inner vital energy. Although of small build, she has fully developed breasts and long hair which reaches down to her knees. Above all, she is warm "like a little stove" and thus capable of warming and energizing the world around her:

In the morning when she jumped out of bed, the heat of her body agreeably expelled the chill of the north room. She plunged her arms into the wash basin, pushed her leg into pants and socks, lifted it on to a chair to button up her shoes—with every movement a warm breath went into the atmosphere; the surroundings were comfortably warmed for her.

Thus, never driven to haste by frost and shivers, she found time to look in the mirror while dressing, to peer under her hair, into her throat, to brush her teeth thoroughly. (*G*, 4:79)

This passage is meant to give an impression of Meta's vitality. It describes her as a source of energy and explains her various actions in the light of this one characteristic. The result of this narrative perspective is, to a certain extent, the breakup of the conventional concept of the individual. Meta is seen less as a person and more as a robot, whose singular parts can be set into singular motions: arms are flung, legs are pushed or raised. All these motions follow from one cause and produce one basic effect: heat.

Growing up is, at least in the ideal case, a process in which such "heat" is accumulated, and the adult should, therefore, resemble a well-charged battery. The fact is, however, that at some point in his life the average person is cut off from the vital power both within and without himself and thus forced to live on a reduced amount of energy. Hence the necessity, felt by most people, to economize, to balance input and output; hence, too, the boredom of ordinary life and the frustrations of a writer in search of "striking personalities."

The reasons given in Sternheim's novellas for this flight into a saver's mentality are varied. In the novella "Vanderbilt," for instance, Sternheim tells the story of a married couple whose life suffers from a blatant disproportion between means and aspirations. Mr. and Mrs. Printz, the two central characters of the novella, aspire to the position of small-town dandies and art connoisseurs. Their financial means are, however, limited, and they perpetually live on the verge of bankruptcy. Rigid saving is the only answer they can find to solve their difficulty, and they end up economizing not only with money but also with their emotions, with the expressions of their individuality, and even with their thoughts. With the help of cosmetics they preserve the appearance of youth; their makeup, however, turns their faces into masks. Similarly, they abstain from forming opinions or expressing judgments of their own. "With 30,000 marks in annuities . . . they could not afford their own judgment" (G, 4:246). All they can do is to reel off their speeches in the manner of record players; the records, however, become increasingly cracked and squeaky. Their ideal in life is to achieve a perfect balance in their energy household since only such a balance can, in their opinion, prevent the exhaustion of their financial and vital resources:

Their expenses for food and living were calculated to the last penny; in the same way they took no more notice of outside sensations than seemed absolutely necessary. For they both idolized life and sought to prolong the duration of their earthly existence by strictly controlling their psychomotor behavior. They had achieved such a level of adaptation that the laughter at their meals harmonized with the sheen of their silver ware and crystal, that the tone of a bad mood did not deviate from the tint of their furniture. (*G*, 4:249)

In other cases, indeed in most, the exhaustion of a person's energy is brought about by acts of social repression. Through its elaborate system of taboos, rules, and interdictions, through its influence on the individual's imagination and through its competitiveness, existing society impairs the natural process of energy accumulation. This is true especially for women who find themselves at the mercy of their male lovers or husbands. Before women reach their thirtieth birthday, their husbands have

tanned their hides and thrown the rest on the dung heap. In the hands of those career makers, not one woman had won the slightest thing, not one had put on an ounce of intellectual flesh. Their souls had been the drain for middle-class waste, their elastic little bodies the drain for masculine vacuousness. Their skin was notched by scars; they could only wait for the knacker. (*G*, 4:118)

The fate of the ordinary male is not necessarily different. In the novella "Busekow," Sternheim enumerates a series of social repressions which turn a human being into a sluggishly burning machine. At school, Busekow had been a slow learner and his first pubertarian urge—during church service he pulled a girl's braids—led to a stern reprimand from the authorities. In later years, his low intelligence prevented him from pursuing a petty career in the army; he had to join the police instead. Here he is handicapped by his poor vision. Busekow succeeds, however, in turning this handicap into an asset. By concentrating all his energy on the development of his eyesight and his attentiveness, he becomes one of the most reliable watchmen of the squad. Yet the older he grows, the more he has to economize in this field too. "Conscious of his resources," he had, in the beginning, "wasted the capital of his eyesight on the world around him" (*G*, 4:8). Now he has to invest his capital cautiously, and he gives passers-by the "credit of his attention" only if he does not know them. He is, in this respect, the opposite of a banker, who gives the most credit to those whom he knows best (*G*, 4:8). Even worse, however, by turning into an eye machine, Busekow has weakened his physical strength and his potency. He has not succeeded in making his wife pregnant and always has to think of the debts which he owes her (*G*, 4:22). When confronting his wife he consequently exhibits feelings of utter humiliation and self-annihilation. At night he curls his fingers around the sides of his bed in order to avoid any physical contact with her. Both he and his wife talk to each other as sparingly as possible: "they economized in their glances and in their talk" (*G*, 4:11).

Those who economize by fleeing into a life of routine, the stories go on, always end up on the losing side. Vital or financial expenses finally drain the remaining resources. The would-be savers live on their capital rather than on their interest; their development thus reaches a point where life turns into a slow death. Their actions become mechanized, routine replaces spontaneity, and their energy trickles out of them like water from a hose "which is not tight any more" (*G*, 4:152). To live on in this way, to "be ashamed of even smoldering" (*G*, 4:111), characterizes the average existence. Sternheim's heroes, however, are not average; their biographies are worth telling because they do not submit to this common fate. Their experiences generally lead to a feeling of utter dejection followed by an outburst of hatred; and hatred is one of the antidotes—not the only one as will be seen—against lethargy and death. He who hates is at least self-centered and self-conscious in his attitudes and thus capable of surviving. On the other hand, hatred is not seen in Sternheim's stories as a truly productive force. It does not help man to rediscover the lost sources of his own natural vitality, but only turns him into an exploiter of others, into one who taps the energy of his fellow human beings. Sternheim's novellas thus repeat, although with a different metaphorical system, certain structural elements which were central to his plays. The observer and director who made others act for his pleasure is now described as a vampire feeding on the life blood of those around him.

The most blatant example of a story built upon the dialectics of the victim turning master can be found in the novella "Schuhlin." The hero of this novella has only one goal in life: to get rid of the stigma attached to his proletarian background and to become, through his musical creations, a center of attention and an object of general admiration. He soon realizes, however, that he is admired only as long as he can present novelties to the public, and that his period of success ends as soon as he has used up his powder. Filled with "hatred against mankind and its creator" (*G*, 4:46), he therefore retires from the world, he creeps "more deeply into himself" and thus acquires a mood which gives "him personality and a superior position" (*G*, 4:52). Above all, he learns that his musical talents, although not sufficient to impress the world at large, allow him to exploit a limited group of people to the fullest possible degree. Schuhlin latches onto a woman and a rich young apprentice who are more than willing to sacrifice their money, their energies, and even their lives for him.

At the other end of the social spectrum, the will to exploit others no longer depends on personal experiences but takes on the quality of a quasi-inherited trait. This is the case with Yvette, a wealthy heiress who is comparable to a bird of prey, an "enormous vulture" (*G*, 4:306). Yvette has learned early in life that her money can buy anything, including, for instance, the sexual potency of her male servants. It is with this attitude too that she approaches business affairs. Her father's old-fashioned attempt to keep up an air of respectability and moderation in his business dealings seems completely illogical to her. There is, according to the novella, only one phenomenon in life which is not accessible to buying power: the pleasurable and energizing stimuli originating from works of art. Yvette can, of course, surround herself with any painting she may desire; yet she has no antenna for the fascinating qualities of artistic beauty. She tries to overcome this deficiency by acquiring a poet named Rainer Maria Bland whom she exploits as a source of both sexual and literary energies.[3] She starts collecting his sentiments in the form of letters and poems and when she has "three volumes" in her hands, she dismisses him: "When their affair drew to an amicable close, the smirking corners of her mouth revealed her triumph over a totally plundered man. She

viewed him as the empty sack which crumples in a corner" (G,
4:310).

Critics have observed that the social relationships presented in
Sternheim's works are characterized by the universal will to power,
and that the realistic quality of his oeuvre is based on his ability to
uncover the hidden motivations governing the actions of his contemporaries.[4] The examples given so far seem to substantiate this
interpretation. Birds of prey and empty sacks, vampires and living
shadows: these are the roles which society offers to its members. It
has also become obvious, however, that the aesthete Sternheim
does not allow his writings to be governed by any wrath against
the exploiters. On the aesthetic level they appear more attractive to
him than those average nonentities who have abdicated their
willpower and vital energies. And yet, in spite of this prevailing
contempt for the victims, Sternheim is anything but an advocate of
bourgeois—or Nietzschean—ruthlessness. He knows and demonstrates that a universalized system of exploitation must needs result
in the diminution of the aesthetic qualities of the world.[5] Exploiters are nonproductive or, to revert to the system of energy dynamics, they have access only to limited and secondary sources of vital
power. In the same degree as they monopolize energy, they destroy
it and end up turning the rest of the world into a dull gray.

It is for this reason that Sternheim, in his plays, supplanted his
original hymn on the ruthless bourgeois with the call for a general
cultural revolution or at least for a reorientation of the lives of individuals. In his novellas the same tendency is dominant from the
very beginning. Most of Sternheim's chronicles do not end at the
point at which life becomes either a matter of routine or of exploitation. They proceed by hinting at a new stage of existence, one at
which the individual, rather than depending on his exploitative instincts and on his ability to abuse others, recharges the batteries of
his life by rediscovering the potentials of energy and pleasure hidden either in his own body or in the objects around him. Mrs.
Printz—to give a few examples of this utopian dimension of
Sternheim's stories—solves the crisis of her life by purchasing a
dandy's reliquary, a fashionable hat, which for her and her husband
becomes a source of incessant fascination; Busekow falls in love

with a prostitute, who helps him to rediscover both his self-esteem and his sexual potency; and the end of the novella "Yvette" shows not the victory of the "vulture" but rather the triumph of her former victim, the poet Bland. Bland meets a woman who is an "electric current" and who can "recharge" his organism. To quote a sentence which defines Sternheim's concept of existential reorientation in more general terms, the experience of love makes him "fluidly human after a life spent with formulae and concepts" (*G*, 4:312).[6]

Sternheim's Narrative Style

In his essay "Tasso or the Art of the Juste Milieu," Sternheim launches an all-out attack against those "bespectacled schmucks" who "invented the label 'grotesque' " in order to take the sting out of writings generated by "ardent wrath and by the urge to revolutionize both middle-class literature and a senile form of life" (*G*, 4:194). The sentence refers to Georg Büchner, the most radical revolutionary among nineteenth-century German authors. Indirectly, however, it also applies to Sternheim's own writings[7] and to the public's reception of them. Sternheim's comedies had been interpreted as satires, and his novellas were cited by critics as prime examples of a grotesque style of narration. In Sternheim's eyes the two labels, "grotesque" and "satirical," signaled a conspiracy. They allowed the public to ignore the most important aspect of his oeuvre: its revolutionizing potential.

Subsequent critics have participated in this conspiracy for seemingly good reasons.[8] Sternheim's novellas present a world which, at least initially, seems to be dissociated and fragmented. Persons appear on the same level as machines, artistic products are equated with coins in a piggy bank, a fashionable hat produces effects normally associated only with sacred relics. Such ill-fitting combinations, comparisons, and metaphors clearly seem to serve the purpose of disorienting the reader, an effect which is normally ascribed to the grotesque style. Yet it can be shown that the final goal of such narrative devices is, in this case, a constructive one. On the one hand, Sternheim's narrative technique is a late off-shoot of nineteenth-century realism or, more precisely, it stands within a literary tradition which attempts to give an inside presentation of the notion of reality held by various representatives of society. On the other hand, it has to be seen as part of the revolutionizing strategy of the vitalist: by destroying the normal concepts of reality, the narrator Sternheim hopes to set free the energetic and pleasurable potential thought to be hidden "within the atoms" of single phenomena (*G*, 6:34). A few passages from the novellas *Ulrike* and *Busekow* exemplify these procedures.

At the beginning of *Ulrike* the narrator scans the scene of his heroine's early life. The mansion in which she lives is decayed—the fourth window on the first floor is broken—the surrounding park is a sand pit, the sky has a leaden color, and the fields look slimy and yellowish. Then the narrator's camera focuses on the people who live in the house. They are Prussian and Protestant. The family structure is highly patriarchal; their food is monotonous:

Aller Mahlzeiten Beginn und Schluss hiess Gebet. Brot, Schwein und Kartoffel lagen inmitten. Das und die Familie war protestantisch. Preusse der liebe Gott. Evangelisch war Magd Knecht Vieh und alles sehr in den Herrn gekehrt. Über der Gemüter fader Landschaft lag des Hausherrn Zufriedenheit in Kindern und Gesinde als Licht, als Sturm und Gewitter sein Unwille.

Beginning and end of all meals was named prayer. Bread, pork, and potato lay in between. That and the family were Protestant. The good Lord, Prussian. Maid, servant, ox, and ass were Protestant and everything was strictly devoted to the Lord. Over the dull landscape of their minds the master's contentment hovered as a light, his anger as storm and thunder.

There can be no question but that these sentences arrange their material in a manner which violates a reader's normal sense of reality. The father's moods are indistinguishable from the weather, servants and livestock are given highly unfitting denominators, religious and patriotic feelings are merged, prayers appear on the same level as pork and potatoes. And yet it is a realistic intention which structures these equations. Their main purpose is to give an inside view of the manner in which Ulrike, the child of a Prussian Junker, perceives the world around her.

How does such a child register the daily meals? They are a recurring unalterable series of events consisting of the following individual items: prayer, bread, pork, potato, prayer. How would she describe the structure of the universe? God, she would of course answer, is the supreme ruler; but so are the emperor and her father. All of these deities are Protestant; at least two of them are Prussian. Is there a difference between these two qualities? Anything which pertains to the house is subservient to these supreme beings. This is why the daily supper takes on such a rigid, quasi-liturgical form. This can also explain why the difference between animals and servants is negligible. Has she not, furthermore, like all good Protestants, memorized the Tenth Commandment which forbids her to covet her neighbor's "Weib, Knecht, Magd, Vieh"?

The structure of Ulrike's world is comparatively simple. She lives within a well-ordered cosmos in which every object has its preordained place. Each glance at this world—and each sentence, no matter how short—reaffirms the same structure. The policeman Busekow, by contrast, has to live in a world of high complexity and, more important, faces an insoluble dilemma which turns his life into constant battle. By consequence, the sentences which describe his life are long and intricate; they lead toward illusory goals and have to relate an almost infinite number of conditions and consequences, actions and reactions, hopes and disappointments:

Von einem tüchtigen Menschen war die Schlappe der Geburt, Kurzsichtigkeit, zu einem Vorteil für sich umgebogen worden, hatte er, seiner Nichteignung für eine Aufsichtsstellung im Urteil zuständiger Instanzen gewiss, alle gesunden Kräfte von anderen Organen ins Auge hochziehend, diesen hinter Gläsern so schneidigen Ausdruck verliehen, dass die befugten Personen erklärten, sie erwarteten Besonderes von seinem scharfen Hinsehen. Er wiederum besorgt, er möchte diese Hoffnung enttäuschen, wandelte, den Körper immer mehr vergewaltigend, im Lauf der Zeiten die gesamte Barschaft an praller Muskelkraft in Späh- und Spürvermögen um, bis seine Schenkel, die unter dem Sergeanten des fünfzigsten Infanterieregimentes gewaltige Tagmärsche zurückgelegt hatten, ihn saftlos und schlapp auf Posten kaum mehr hielten, die einst vom Gewehrstrecken geschwellten Arme Lust leidenschaftlichen Zugreifens verloren.

A capable man had twisted the blow received at birth, shortsightedness, to his own advantage; certain of the fact that the proper authorities would deem him unfit for supervisory positions, he had, by drawing all healthy energies from the other organs up into his eyes, conferred upon these such a trenchant expression, behind glasses, that the authorized persons declared they expected something exceptional from his perspicacity. Apprehensive that he might disappoint these hopes, he in turn, doing more and more violence to his body, exchanged all his ready cash of bulging muscle into probing and tracking powers to the point that his thighs, which, under the command of the sergeant of the fiftieth infantry regiment, had marched enormous distances but which were now sapless and sagging, scarcely held him at his post any longer and to the point that his arms, once swelled from presenting the rifle, lost all the joy of passionate grasping. (*G*, 4:7)

Once again, it is, above all, an inside view of the hero's existence which is conveyed by these sentences. There had once been a time when Busekow had registered individual phenomena as sources of joy, and the narrator who follows his hero's perspective as closely as possible attempts to be precise in naming such items. Busekow was proud not of his muscular strength in general or even of his legs but of his thighs, which had grown strong not just in military service but through particular exercises done in a unique regiment under the command of a specific sergeant.

The world in which the policeman lives at present is, unfortunately, structured quite differently. It is a machinery governed by rules of functional adequacy. Expectations must be met, bodies must fit certain tasks, defects in one area must be balanced by achievements in another. Those who have the power to apply these rules use such phrases as "Nichteignung für eine Aufsichtsstellung," "Urteil zuständiger Instanzen," "die befugten Personen erklärten," bureaucratic phrases capable of producing nightmares. Such sentences register only the functions which a person can or cannot fulfill; they leave room neither for the concept of individuality nor for that of organic units. The hero, who possesses a machine of his own, his body, must apply the same rules. This body consists of a number of interchangeable and alterable parts some of which are marred by a defect, his shortsightedness. Such shortcomings, to be sure, can be corrected through the reallocation of energies which a person has at his disposal. The strength of arms and legs can be transformed into "eye power," an obvious deficit can be turned into an apparent asset. The social machinery, however, is equally flexible. Its demands increase as soon as its initial expectations are met, which, in turn, requires a set of new adjustments on the part of the hero. Busekow is thus caught in an infinite web in which every seeming improvement only worsens the situation.

It cannot be denied that such a description seems to contain a number of grotesque features. These features, however, occur in a completely systematized form; and, far from conveying an impression of fragmentation and distortion, they amount to a thoroughly structured narrative universe. Busekow's body, for instance, does not seem to be alive. It is a thing which can be shaped, modeled and remodeled almost *ad libitum*, it is a thing of wax rather than of flesh. Seen from a physiological point of view, the transformations of his body are certainly implausible. They are, however, totally adequate and logical within the system of energy exploitation which gives the first part of the novella its overall structure.

This simultaneity of surface dissociation and inner coherence, which is characteristic of the above passage, also characterizes the ending of the novella which relates Busekow's escape from the net in which he had so far been entangled. The hero meets the prostitute Gesine and, in the course of his love affair, he rediscovers new sources of energy which permit him to change his entire concept of himself and of the world around him. He finds out that he is sexually potent, he remembers elements of his long forgotten Protestant religion, and he learns how to put his nationalism, a prerequisite for his job, to good use. At the peak of their sexual ecstasies, Gesine starts reciting the names of Adam and Abraham, Saul and David, and the other biblical heroes and thus manages further to enflame the ardor of Busekow's love.

Moses David Jesus und alle Helden des Buches war Christof in dieser Nacht. Es strömte heroische Männlichkeit von Jahrtausenden aus ihm. Sie nahm hin und schmeichelte ihm hold, dass keine Kraft aus seinen Lenden wich, er hochgemut bis zum Morgen blieb, als sie in leichten

Schlummer verzaubert sank. Da riss er sich von ihr, reckte die Brust in den Tag, fand sich ans Klavier. Hingezogen von Gefühlen, suchend hoch-reissend aus Erinnerung, drückte er mit einem Finger in die Tasten: Heil dir im Siegerkranz! Und mit Stimme folgend, mächtiger anschwellend, variierte er über beiden Pedalen vom Bass bis in höchsten Diskant—da klang es ihm selig:

> Heil dir im Siegerkranz
> Fühl in des Thrones Glanz
> die hohe Wonne ganz
> Heil Kaiser dir.

That night Christof was Moses David Jesus and all the heroes of the book. Heroic virility of millenia was streaming out of him. She accepted and ca-ressed him sweetly so that the strength of his loins was left intact and he remained high spirited till morning when she enchantedly fell into a light slumber. Then he tore himself away, flung out his chest toward the dawn, found his way to the piano. Drawn by emotion, searching, seizing from the depth of memory, he pressed the keys with one finger: *Heil dir im Siegerkranz*. And continuing vocally, swelling ever more mightily, he varied the music with both pedals from bass to highest treble—and lo, it sounded blissful. . . . (*G*, 4:25)

If Busekow, in this scene, conceives himself as a reincarnation of masculinity and heroism, the narrator certainly does his best to support this view. Such words as "hold," "Kraft der Lenden," and "hochgemut", are reminiscent of the language used by Luther or in the medieval heroic epic. The sequence "Da riss er sich los . . ." reproduces the gestures which express the hero's triumphant feel-ings. His attempt to intone the national anthem on the piano is described as a reawakening of the hidden and deadened layers of his psyche; awkward and subdued at first, it ends in a glorious cres-cendo, a musical orgasm.

This narrative device, the merging of the hero's and the narra-tor's perspective, might, of course, be interpreted as highly ironic. It is easily understood, furthermore, that the juxtaposition of low values—sex with a prostitute—and high ones—religion and pa-triotism—has struck many critics as satirical if not blasphemous. It is equally obvious, however, that such evaluations are based on abstract categories of value which cannot be found in the story itself. These interpretations become implausible, therefore, as soon as the reader follows the narrator's invitation and sees the world from the point of view of the hero. By quoting the Bible, the two lovers do not ridicule religion, but instead rediscover it for themselves. Throughout his life, Busekow had experienced such cultural institutions as the church or the government as social instruments of oppression. In the above scene, he finds out for the first time that both the patriarchs and the emperor in his victorious pose are worth remembering and citing as embodiments of virile strength. They are worth remembering, furthermore, because he, the lowly Busekow, has become their equal. Busekow, in other words, has discovered the pleasurable potential of cultural images. Used in this way, as stimuli of joy, their existence can obviously be justified.

The above observations can easily be generalized. An ardent admirer of Flaubert,[9] Sternheim tells his stories without recourse to the subjective and evaluative interferences of a personal narrator. He thus describes not one world but a multitude of perceptual systems whose particular nature depends on the point of view of a particular hero. Ulrike, the Protestant girl, perceives the universe in the form of a patriarchal family; the policeman Busekow finds himself confronted with a system of functional equations; freed from his burdens, he suddenly lives in the midst of innumerable sources of pleasure and energy. In all such cases, Sternheim does not, however, describe fleeting and coincidental impressions, but he presents universes of a highly systematic, coherent, and quasi-objective character. Moreover, in all such cases he tends to disregard conventional forms of perception and conventional hierarchies of value, a tendency which is especially noticeable as soon as his heroes turn into emancipated hedonists. That which cultural conventions degrade as trivial and lowly may give more pleasure to man than those values which are praised for their significance and greatness. Or conversely, it may be the hedonist's goal to reduce those supposedly sublime values, which are beyond the reach of the normal mortal, in such a way as to turn them into sources of enjoyment. Sternheim's equation of the base and the sublime—a narrative device which he uses abundantly in his prose—is thus not an expression of satire or blasphemy but a consequence of the unreserved application of the pleasure principle. Pleasure has, in Sternheim's stories as well as in his social theory, a function which is normally ascribed to money: it acts as the great equalizer and thus eliminates hierarchical structures.

Revolutionizing Narration

As long as the narrator Sternheim sets up a particular scene, or as long as he reproduces the view of the world held by one of his heroes, he attempts to act as an impartial and neutral medium of narration. This impartiality is, however, not unlimited. The various ways of perceiving reality are not considered equally valid; they may allow more or less freedom, offer more or less pleasure, and, above all, may either bar or open access to the energy of the universe. Taken as a whole, therefore, each of Sternheim's novellas betrays the existence of an author who, far from being neutral, clearly propagates an idea: hedonistic vitalism.

The various philosophical systems of vitalism share at least one central premise: they are based on a complete disregard for the working sphere as the basis of all social life. In Sternheim's case this is especially noticeable. Once his heroes are emancipated, they tend to perceive the world as it might appear to a newborn child, to a stockholder or, perhaps, to the ideal affluent consumer contemplating the offerings of the market. Nature and society seem to consist of an indefinite number of "sources" in which energy automatically accrues and from which it can be withdrawn at any moment. The illusory character of this concept is almost self-evident. Neither the creation of a work of art—for Sternheim an inexhaustible "stock of voluptuous powers" (*G*, 4:305)—nor the growth of a human body—interpreted as the individual's primary energy machine—nor even the ripening of an edible apple are in any way automatic processes. They are all dependent on the input of human labor.

A social philosopher who considers work the primary source of social energy can easily explain the existence of exploitative relationships. If, by contrast, energy is thought to be a natural and quantitatively unlimited resource, then the phenomenon of exploitation becomes almost inexplicable. Why, it must then be asked, does a human being, instead of accepting those "sources" which are freely offered, resort to tapping the energy of others? To resolve this paradox, vitalist thinkers have generally posited an objective dualism within the structure of the world. The fluid, flowing, and creative powers of life, they claim, are involved in a struggle with their ontological opponent, inert, inanimate matter.[10] The eternal foe of life—and of human happiness—thus appears in various forms: in the form of dikes which channel and strangle the floods of life, of crusts which imprison fiery nuclei, of cinders which prevent a fire from burning, or of walls which encage man's free vision. In the socio-cultural sphere the same foe is to be found in anything which impairs the spontaneity of man's experiences, thoughts, and actions: in epistemological categories, in established beliefs and cultural traditions, in social institutions, and in hierarchical systems of value.[11] All these are considered the petrifications of social life which tend to cut man off from the original sources of vital power and force him either to save limited amounts of energy or to exploit his fellow beings. The reinstitution of human freedom or—in Sternheim's words—of a state of existence in which man is "fluidly human after a life spent with formulae and concepts" (*G*, 4:312) would thus require a quasi-permanent revolution of man's thoughts and habits or at least a revolutionizing act strong enough to wash away dikes and walls and to cleanse out the arteries of life.

To contribute to this revolutionizing process is, according to Sternheim's wartime essays, one of the major tasks of literature. Most contemporary writers, Sternheim argues, have failed in this respect: they have contented themselves with reshuffling existing values along preestablished hierarchical lines, and they thus leave untouched the very structure of traditional perceptual habits. A truly radical writer would have to do more. To be "a real liberator" he would have to "blast away the old slogans and to establish new and valid elements." To illustrate this emancipatory potential of literature, Sternheim repeatedly points to Gottfried Benn's poetry.

Benn, he says, "revolts from within the atoms, not on the surface" (*G*, 6:34).[12] Another such literary revolutionary is the expressionist novelist Kasimir Edschmid. "Like me and partly even more strongly than me," Sternheim addresses him in a congratulatory letter, "you dash to pieces the limiting crust of concepts and make them reexplode from within" (*G*, 6:103).[13]

In the novella "Meta," Sternheim has integrated this concept of "revolutionizing narration" into the plot line of the story. At the end of her life, after a series of successful attempts at giving vent to her explosive personality, the heroine of this story gathers around herself a group of older women, of "twenty souls paled in average lives, exhausted little flames which were afraid of even smoldering," whom she manages to inspire with new life:

Meta stormed into them with youth and heavenly conviction. She wound back the film of their lives, she pointed out the frequent high points, she showed each of them the incomparable quality of their earthly strivings. In faded bosoms she ignited a belated, yet perfect conviction of the unique importance of that for which they had bloomed. (*G*, 4:111)

Evidently, the significance of these sentences goes beyond their specific meaning within the story. By describing the effects which a narrator can have on his public, they hint at the intention which Sternheim pursued in writing his own stories. Meta's narrations are meant to reconstruct the biographies of her audience; they are told, however, in such a way as to give meaning to seemingly futile existences and to transform into a series of dramatic events that which had appeared to be commonplace. The listeners thus reexperience their own lives as a drama and—consequently—as a source of pleasure.

This, however, is a rare example. In general, Sternheim refrains from turning his literary intentions into a topic of his own narrative. Instead, he heavily emphasizes another "vitalizing" phenomenon: sexuality. Even more, he uses the various manifestations of love as narrative symbols to describe different forms of human interaction. Sex can occur in the form of rape and prostitution and thus mirror exploitative relationships; presented as a mutual exchange of pleasure, it can stand for a utopian existence in which man is simultaneously a source and a receptacle of energy; it can also be described as a violently beneficial act leading to a cleansing of body and soul. There is indeed hardly a novella which does not make abundant use of erotic descriptions—a fact which did not fail to attract the wrath of Wilhelminian censors[14]—and there is hardly a sexual manifestation which Sternheim did not, in one way or another, integrate into his system of energy dynamics.

Seen as a mirror of social life, sexuality transcends the level of the merely personal. It appears as a vitalizing force of wide significance, as an image of a general rejuvenation of man's existence. It is evident, however, that the emancipatory potential of lovemaking is void of any historical specification; it develops its effects regardless of social or political circumstances. The same shortcoming is characteristic of the philosophy of vitalism in general. The posited dualism between the stream of life and inert matter is an ontological one; its historically specific forms are coincidental and secondary in importance.

Up to this point, Sternheim's novellas might thus appear as dealing with the so-called eternal problems of human existence or—in other words—they might be considered products of a writer who is oblivious of the specific events of his time. Yet such an impression would be highly misleading. While Sternheim is certainly interested in the ontological aspects of vitalistic images, he also attempts to bring forth their time-bound potential. Since he interprets both a person's biography and human history as an incessant series of changes, of innovations and revolutions, he is bound to ask for the specific directions into which an individual's life or a social system is to evolve at any given moment. Without doubt, Sternheim intends his novellas to give an answer to this question or, at least, he intends them to be adequate reflections of social changes and social possibilities brought about by the war and to be indicators of a necessary reorientation of social life. It is thus no coincidence that many of his stories owe a good deal of their explosive symbolism to the experiences of World War I and that his narrative theory is both a response to the breakdown of Wilhelminian society and an attempt to anticipate the ensuing political revolution. In a limited number of Sternheim's novellas, furthermore, the effects of the war have a direct impact on the biographies told,[15] and at least one of them, "Heidenstam," is an attempt to combine biographical narration with the depiction of specific historical changes. In aesthetic terms, the novella contrasts an impressionist and an expressionist view of the world; in social terms it describes the transition from prewar capitalism to that which, towards the end of the war, became Sternheim's great hope: a society based on anarcho-aesthetic principles.

"Heidenstam" starts with reconstructing the world view of a wealthy stock owner. Drawing 42,000 marks in yearly dividends, Heidenstam can indeed have the impression of living in a *perpetuum mobile* and of having access to an inexhaustible source of energy. Money invested regenerates money in ever-increasing amounts. There may be incalculable setbacks in one economic field; these are, however, outweighed by gains in others. The question as to how these profits are produced does not enter Heidenstam's mind. His intellect does not penetrate the surface level of the stock exchange, and, according to the novella, Heidenstam could not even afford to acquire any in-depth knowledge of his investments. It is only the economic system in its entirety which produces dividends in a reliable manner; each individual item can always, and for no good reason, turn out to be a failure. It would thus be a sheer waste of energy to investigate the qualities of any particular object. Heidenstam consequently develops an "impressionistic" relationship to his surroundings (*G*, 4:164). He allows himself to be impressed only by superficial sensations; he can only scan the surface of things and he has to hurry from one moment, from one fleeting impression to the next.

This scanning of surfaces—in Sternheim's terms, this disregard for the energetic nuclei of individual objects—works only in periods of economic boom. It produces catastrophic results as soon as the market loses its character of a *perpetuum mobile*, that is, in times of war and of economic crisis. Shortly after the outbreak of World War I, Heidenstam thus has to go through a profound learning process. He realizes that, by defining his own person and the objects around him both in terms of exchange and as functions of a fluctuating market structure, he has allowed himself to be encaged in a limited and unreliable system of energy. He further learns—and this is Sternheim's message for the bourgeois—that he needs to rediscover the inexhaustible aesthetic qualities inherent in any particular object of the world.

The war which has brought about Heidenstam's existential crisis now also helps him find a new formula for his existence. Heidenstam experiences war as a great fireworks and realizes that each living thing—from his wife down to the stray dogs roaming the streets and to the potatoes buried in the furrows—resembles a colorful firecracker. Stimulated by so much explosiveness around him, he himself turns into an explosive. He becomes a manic war enthusiast, not, to be sure, of the chauvinistic, but of the anarcho-aesthetic kind. He has no interest in countries to be annexed, in national honors to be restored, or in battles to be won. Instead, he enthusiastically extols the aesthetics of explosions. Since society cannot tolerate this attitude, he is finally locked up in an insane asylum. Here, however, he finds an atmosphere which totally fits his newly discovered aesthetic needs. The asylum is populated by maniacs, "real characters" who have no other interest in life but to act out their own inner drives to the fullest degree and regardless of either inner inhibitions or outer social constraints.

War as the father of a new and free aesthetic perception, the insane asylum as the model of utopian society: it need not be emphasized that such presentations contain a large element of irony. It is, however, the irony of exaggeration which does not preclude the basic seriousness of these suggestions. Nietzsche's dictum that the world can only be justified as an aesthetic phenomenon is one of the implicit centers of Sternheim's *vision du monde*. Fighting and the will to exploit others, Sternheim argues, are prevalent only within societies which prevent individuals from realizing the aesthetic energies of the universe. Individuals who have access to the unlimited vital sources of the objective world can have no possible interest in subduing each other. In doing so, they would only deprive themselves of possible sources of pleasure. A free society, according to Heidenstam's insights, would thus be one in which eccentrics coexist and stimulate each other to reach their highest potential. It is for this reason that the insane asylum can achieve a utopian meaning. Within its walls, social interaction is character-ized by the same mutuality which made sexual intercourse a model of emancipation. All the detained patients are, at the same time, actors and spectators, sources and recipients of pleasure. Or, seen from a different perspective, the utopian world of the asylum is one where the principles of comedy have been universalized.

Sternheim does not fail to mention the fact that there is one en-trance requirement to this paradise: the checking account. Or, more generally speaking, in this as in other cases, Sternheim's uto-pian world—the *perpetuum mobile* of energy and pleasure—rests on the assumption that man is freed from providing the means of his own subsistence. Utopia based on the illusions of an upper-class stockholder? Such a formula might seem appropriate at this point. Yet, despite its partial validity, it would be a shortsighted evalua-tion of Sternheim's literary imagination. The hope that in the fu-ture man will be capable of freeing himself from the need to work is not restricted to particular social classes, nor can it be dismissed as simply illusionary. In fact, there is hardly a utopian thinker in modern times who does not base his concepts on this hope.

The history of the last fifty or sixty years, while enlarging the material and technological basis for man's emancipation from work, has made the social realization of such dreams appear to be more unrealistic than ever. The present period is, in consequence, not a fertile ground for the development, or even the understand-ing of utopian concepts. In this respect it is the direct opposite of the wartime era and its immediate aftermath, of a time in which a radical change of social structures seemed both necessary and easily possible. Seen within this context, Sternheim is but one of a very large and diffuse group of writers who were united by one goal: to envision and establish a society in which labor and exploitation have ceased to determine the structure of man's life. The next chapter will briefly discuss Sternheim's position with regard to such radical groups. The former Wilhelminian aesthete, it will be shown, could quite easily and naturally turn into a sympathizer and advocate of leftist radicalism.

Chapter Nine

The Postwar Years

In Search of New Heroes

For the playwright Sternheim the war years were a period of enforced hibernation. The Prussian government had banned most of his plays as potential sources of public unrest,[1] and directors were reluctant to stage the others. It was partly for this reason that Sternheim, in these years, resorted to writing narrative prose on the one hand and making stage adaptations of older plays on the other.[2] With the end of the war, this situation changed. Two of his plays, *1913* and *Tabula Rasa*, could now be staged for the first time; the other ones were successfully restaged, and Sternheim could once again return to his original literary medium, the theater. In the period between 1920 and 1926, he completed an average of one play per year. This time, however, his talent as a playwright proved to be barren. In the opinion of most critics, it was a new and decidedly inferior Sternheim who now emerged, a playwright who combined a surprising degree of theatrical incompetence with an equally unheard-of amount of personal arrogance. Sternheim answered such attacks in terms of equal vituperation. The result was that, by 1925, he had become *persona non grata* among practically all the literary circles of the Weimar republic. According to a sarcastic rumor, circulated in 1926, he had died toward the end of the war and his later publications were nothing but the products of an inept twin brother.[3]

It would be futile to defend the late Sternheim against such cruel criticism. His postwar plays do indeed offer little that is of lasting interest. Above all, they document both Sternheim's unrelenting ambition—to be received as a mentor of the German public—and, at the same time, his decided insecurity in the face of the historical change which had been brought about by World

War I. As paradoxical as this may seem, some of the weaknesses of Sternheim's later plays are due to his growing political concerns and political insights. As has been shown earlier, his prewar comedies rested on one central premise. They drew a sharp line between existing middle-class ideologies and fantasies on the one hand and bourgeois pragmatism on the other, a pragmatism which Sternheim interpreted as a potential source of hedonistic pleasure and individualistic emancipation. Although such distinctions and interpretations can be considered dubious and naive, they nevertheless were highly effective as a stage formula, and they provided the author with an excellent basis for the conception of comic figures. By the end of the prewar period, however, Sternheim had already lost his initial confidence in the overall positive effects of what he called the "bourgeois character." More important even, he now considered middle-class ideology as a necessary off-shoot of capitalism and hence of bourgeois pragmatism. Sofie Maske uses both her financial skills and her brainwashing power for the same purposes. The outbreak of the war and Germany's political reorganization after 1919 further added to Sternheim's increasing disillusionment. He interpreted the initial public support of the war as a necessary result of a long and irrevocable indoctrination process, and he remained equally hostile to the final establishment of a democratic system in Germany. To be sure, postwar Germany was freed of many of its feudal relics, and the bourgeoisie had, in a way, won its battle against the aristocracy. At the same time, however, the country was farther removed than ever from breaking the chains of what Sternheim considered middle-class mentality. Sternheim, from now on, deemed it utterly impossible to portray the new German bourgeois in the form of a dramatic hero. If anything, the middle classes had become, in his opinion, historical nonentities and objects of contempt. They were, as he said in one of his plays, "colorless characters, . . . a boom and burst bunch, a miserable lot."[4]

Deprived of his former dramatic personnel, forsaken so to speak by the bourgeoisie—his former audience, his literary discovery and the basis of his historical optimism[5]—the late Sternheim, much like Ernst Stadler in *1913*, finds himself on a continuous search.

He is on the lookout for new model figures, for a type of hero capable of transcending the realm of middle-class mentality. In two of his plays, *The Unchained Contemporary* (1920) and *The Fossil* (1932), Sternheim tries to discover such heroes among the political radicals of his time or, more precisely, among a brand of intellectuals who, after having broken with Marxist or strictly anarchist tenets, were pursuing an "anti-authoritarian" line of action. The three remaining plays, *Manon Lescaut* (a dramatization of Prévost's famous novel), *Oscar Wilde*, and *Uznach School*, follow the same basic model, albeit without political overtones. The heroes presented in all these plays share at least three major characteristics. They no longer represent any social group or social class; instead, they are conceived as "individualists," a fact which results in a noticeable lack of dramatic realism. In contrast to Sternheim's earlier plays, they are youthful figures;[6] and, third, they prove their exemplary qualities by being or becoming ardent lovers. With the exception of *The Nebbich*, a satire on the glamor world of the Weimar republic, Sternheim's postwar plays center around one basic theme: they show how the victorious power of love overcomes social persecutions as well as the barriers of differing political, philosophical, and cultural convictions.

Sternheim's contemporary critics found it impossible to understand, let alone appreciate, this unexpected "romanticizing" turn.[7] Was not Sternheim, they asked, propagating the same outworn middle-class sentimentalities which he had so convincingly denounced in his earlier comedies?[8] There was another, and perhaps even stronger, reason for bewilderment. The same writer who, in his plays, praised the overwhelming power of love, and who seemed to demonstrate the superficial character of political tenets, presented himself as a political radical in his essayistic writings, and he did so not in abstract terms but by actively supporting the Aktionskreis, which had been formed by the journalist and publisher Franz Pfemfert, and which was known to be one of the most radically politicized groups of the time.[9]

Pfemfert had gained his political reputation by organizing the antiwar movement among those German radical intellectuals who had decided not to emigrate from their country. In the months during and after the German revolution, he was allied with the Spartakus-Bund, the nucleus of the German Communist party. This alliance lasted until 1920 when Pfemfert, together with other radicals, was expelled from the party because of his unwillingness to give up his ultracommunist and anarchist convictions. In contrast to the then official policies of the communists, he remained an outspoken opponent of all attempts on the part of radical groups to gain power through parliamentary work and through party organizations. Such attempts, he thought, would only lead to the mental corruption of the workers and thus perpetuate, even after a revolutionary takeover, the old power structures of bourgeois society. Rather than relying on organizational hierarchies, Pfemfert favored a grass roots or "soviet" democracy with local centers which were to be formed in factories and which were to enjoy a high degree of autonomy.

It is not surprising that, with this anarchistic contempt for power structures, the Aktionskreis never gained any political importance. Culturally, on the other hand, its impact was somewhat more relevant. Pfemfert shared the opinion of other ultracommunists that the revolutionary situation of 1918 had arisen before the masses had intellectually grasped the meaning of Marxism.[10] Hence the necessity to stage battles on the cultural front. Again in contrast to the Communist party, which dissociated itself from the literary avant garde and attempted to save the "cultural heritage," the Aktionskreis sided with such movements as the Berlin version of dadaism, and, above all, it advocated a complete break with all the literary and cultural traditions of the bourgeois era.[11]

Sternheim, the dandy, the aesthete, the former owner of Bellemaison and author of romanticizing plays, as a close friend of Franz Pfemfert and as a supporter of radical politics! For the overwhelming majority of his critics this was an outrageous and nonsensical combination. For a present-day reader, who can look at the whole corpus of Sternheim's works, this combination is at least understandable. Throughout his life, Sternheim was a radical of sorts. Although hardly interested in political or economic questions in a narrow sense, he was a proponent of some vaguely defined concept of cultural revolution, and both his belated sympathy for the

Aktionskreis and his presentation of "radical lovers" are in agreement with this general stance. Among the aspects of Pfemfert's program it was, above all, its vehement iconoclasm which Sternheim found most congenial. Quite in tune with both his own established convictions and the philosophy of the Kreis, he thus praised certain representatives of the nineteenth-century anarchist tradition,[12] and he vehemently attacked anything which smacked of bourgeois mentality. Targets of such attacks were Goethe and the nineteenth-century German literary and philosophical tradition, the Social Democratic and Communist parties,[13] the majority of expressionist writers,[14] and finally the whole spectrum of the pre- and postwar literary establishment including all critics, most stage directors, and his own publisher Kurt Wolff. On the other hand, yet in tune with his former convictions, Sternheim showed considerably less interest in questions pertaining to the organization of labor, that is, to the key concern of all genuine anarchist and ultracommunist groups. He did share, at least temporarily, Pfemfert's concern for the workers, and he did write articles which were meant to strengthen their "consciousness"; yet he never considered the proletariat a revolutionary class in the Marxian sense. Instead, he emphasized the workers' anti-authoritarian potential and their supposed freedom from middle-class dementia. As a consequence, Sternheim viewed all symptoms of social integration with the utmost suspicion. The workers, he pointed out, had already been dangerously close to losing their specific character in prewar society, and the increasing stability and prosperity of the Weimar republic was leading, in his opinion, to the same dangerous results.[15] More important, Sternheim saw no reason why his—admittedly limited—sympathy for the workers should prevent him from uncovering the anti-authoritarian energies latent in other social strata, or why it should prevent him from admiring a dandy like Oscar Wilde, a post-Nietzschean poet like Gottfried Benn,[16] or even a right-wing German general.[17] Sternheim's "romanticizing" plays do not contradict, but rather support, this vague and thoroughly individualistic concept of radicalism. Uncompromising love is, in Sternheim's opinion, the highest and clearest symbol of an anti-authoritarian attitude, and even the political radical could meet with his approval only if he managed to be, at the same time, an ardent lover.

In 1925, after Sternheim had completed his drama *Oscar Wilde*, the members of the Aktionskreis finally realized that Sternheim's particular version of radicalism was not compatible with their own political convictions. Sternheim was expelled from this group and thus also deprived of an important medium for publication. One year later he staged one last play,[18] *Uznach School*. The relative success which this comedy enjoyed was not sufficient to outweigh his by now definitive literary isolation. Personal problems— Sternheim's marriage with Thea Bauer was dissolved in 1927—and a series of physical and mental illnesses contributed to silencing the author. In 1932, one year before the Nazi takeover, Sternheim emigrated to Brussels, where he lived a life of almost complete isolation until his death in 1942.

The Radical Message

"To make visible the eternal collision between the two forces of reality, reason and ethics" (*G*, 6:201): this is the theoretical formula with which Sternheim, in one of his postwar essays, tries to define the task of the playwright. The laws of reason, according to this formula, pertain to the realms of those natural and social forces which "make of us the humble objects of necessary constraints." He who thinks and acts rationally is "possessed by the world" and deprived of his freedom. He who acts "ethically," according to Sternheim's use of the word, listens only to his own nature. He is a self-determined individual and has won the liberty to follow his own judgments and his innermost drives.

Such distinctions are certainly not new in Sternheim's works. In his early period, when he had been under the influence of the neo-Kantian philosopher Ernst Rickert, Sternheim had already defined the ethical human being as one who stands "above the occurrences of the world" and is thus free to determine his own actions. In Sternheim's comedies, furthermore, it was one of the characteristics of the comic hero that he was capable of drawing a clear line between freedom and necessity. Theobald Maske consents to being the "humble object of necessary constraints" where he is too weak to fight them. This allows him, however, to act freely in his own little niche. Here he can, as he says, "indulge my inclinations, my innermost nature unhindered."

To obey where you must and to be free where you can: this is certainly a trivial and, in political terms, exceedingly conformist answer to the question of freedom and necessity. And yet Sternheim was partly justified when he claimed that his formula provided him with a basis from which he could launch an all-out attack on existing social norms. In Sternheim's thinking, the "two forces of reality, reason and ethics," are not fixed and well-defined entities. The boundaries between them are flexible, and although the individual may never be able to reach a state of complete freedom, he can and should, at any given moment, enjoy a greater amount of liberty than he realizes.

The individual who wants to exploit this potential for freedom to the fullest degree must, however, fulfill two requirements: he not only must see through the various, mostly ideological, mechanisms which society uses to enslave its members, but he must also have a sense of the direction of the historical process since the specific fields in which freedom can be realized are subject to historical change. It follows from this that the playwright, in his role as a promoter of freedom, faces a two-fold task: he must expose the mechanisms of unjustified social repression, and he must be able to point out to his public the specific areas in which an individual can be free within a specific historical period. The playwright must be, in other words, both a critic and a prophet.[19]

European history—this is Sternheim's central critical observation—is characterized by an ever-increasing expansion of the realm of reason and hence by ever-increasing infringements on man's liberty. In his essay *Tasso or the art of the Juste Milieu* Sternheim traces this development in the areas of literature and ideology. The philosophical systems developed by such thinkers as Kant, Hegel, Marx, and Darwin all concur in one point: they interpret the historical process in general, and man's actions in particular, as simple functions of some omnipotent ontological power. This power may be the Kantian voice of morality or the Hegelian self-devel-

opment of reason, it may be the Darwinian law of the survival of
the fittest or a Marxian law of economics. In each case, Sternheim
argues, such philosophical tenets reduce the individual to the size
of a small wheel in a great machine and leave him no choice but
that between total compliance and automatic annihilation.[20]

The literary equivalent of such ideologies is the genre of tragedy
as interpreted by middle-class aesthetic theories. Invariably, the
sad fate of the tragic hero has been to demonstrate the sinister consequences of nonadaptation. The individual desires and drives
which he vehemently expresses at the beginning of the play always
turn out to be misjudgments, flaws of character or violations of
some moral code. Even worse, the typical ending of tragedy presents not only the victory of reason but a hero's voluntary compliance with it. Sternheim goes on to observe that this version of
tragedy, after falling into disrepute in the 1800s, enjoyed a renaissance in World War I expressionist drama. Once again, the literary
ideologists extolled the virtues of compliance, of discipline and
of Christian self-sacrifice. The expressionist glorification of the
"spirit of active love"[21] was, in Sternheim's view, an ideological
tool of oppression.

In a second essay, *Berlin or Juste Milieu*, Sternheim traces the
same developments in the fields of economics, politics, and cultural life. In its most interesting parts, this essay gives a description of the cultural and perceptual changes which resulted from
Germany's abrupt plunge into modern capitalism. Sternheim exposes the myths of the machine and of statistics, the replacement
of individualized production through seemingly autonomous mechanized processes, the concept of "world records" in all cultural,
behavioral, and economic fields, the increasing standardization of
goods which leads to an equal standardization of human activities
and of human taste; he notes the structural equivalence between
the individual's perception of himself as the agent of machines and
the philosophical interpretation of man as a function of economic
and biological processes, and he emphasizes the increasing elimina-
tion of autonomous private realms and the ensuing loss of man's
sense of responsibility in regard to his own actions. Prewar
ideologies thus converged with the daily sensory experiences

brought about by the advance of capitalism and resulted in a thorough change in man's drives, his perceptual categories, and his ethical values.[22]

Many of these observations and arguments are part of the conservative tradition of cultural criticism. In contrast to genuinely conservative authors, however, Sternheim does not glorify earlier historical ages at the expense of later ones. Instead, he invariably and obstinately tries to uncover the emancipatory potential of any given social development. His comedies praised not only the *père de famille*, the older version of the bourgeois hero, but also the social climber and the modern capitalist competitor. Sternheim's later essays pursue a similar line of thought. While deploring the depersonalization of man in modern society, they also emphasize the promising features of cultural changes and thus succeed in describing history as an ambivalent process that has produced ever-greater amounts of both real suppression and potential freedom.

Early twentieth-century middle-class ideology is described by Sternheim as an amalgamate of divergent and mutually exclusive moral and philosophical texts. Ascetic and authoritarian moral concepts were propagated to give support to the capitalist demand for a steady increase of industrial productivity; they prevailed completely in periods of economic depression and in times of war. By contrast, the preparation of war and the pursuit of imperialistic goals resulted in an aggressive and belligerent ideological system. At the same time, economic boom periods furthered the development of hedonistic attitudes. To achieve its basic goal, the increase of profits, the capitalist economy was forced to turn man into an obsessed consumer by providing him with an unparallelled amount of sensory stimulation.

It is in these last-mentioned developments or, in other words, in the anarchical and sensual potential of advanced capitalism that Sternheim tries to uncover the most promising features of twentieth-century history. In his view, the youthful insolence of Wilhelm II, for instance, was not necessarily an early symptom of the country's later imperialistic aggressiveness but rather an expression of the spectator's curiosity. The emperor as well as his young contemporaries were possessed by the drive to find out "what really happened under the sun and where it would shine next" (*G*, 6:117). In the same way, both capitalist consumerism and philosophical systems negating man's social and historical reponsibility could have effected an unheard-of increase in the pleasures of life. Berlin, with its nonexistent cultural tradition, could have been the appropriate place for the development of this new hedonism, and Nietzsche's philosophy could have served as its theoretical basis. There were, according to Sternheim, reasons to hope that the bourgeois, "legitimized by the new doctrine, would indulge in unchained gaiety, in exultant exhilaration," and that, "on the basis of a big bank account," he might "express a Dionysian mood of pure laughter . . . and infect the world with his exuberance."[23]

Dionysian exuberance is the potential of capitalist society— competition, oppression, and the imperialist war as its result! The reason for this disastrous social development, Sternheim says, was the unwillingness of both society in general and its intellectual leaders in particular to break with the ideals, the moral values, and the limited rational concepts which they had inherited from earlier periods. The emperor thus combined the promising "curiosity" with the older version of *Realpolitik*; Nietzsche, who could have been the apostle of Dionysus, ended up praising the will to power; tendencies which could have brought about the emancipation of the human body resulted in the development of competitive sports; the abolition of sexual taboos led to the myth of procreation; instead of unleashing the lust of the consumer, society propagated the increase of productivity. All in all, it was the unbroken tradition of instrumental rationality which prevented the establishment of freedom.

In the prewar period, as a writer of comedies, Sternheim attempted to "cleanse" the imagination of the middle classes from aristocratic allurements. The postwar essayist, confronted with a potentially revolutionary situation, retains both this metaphor and this intention. Now, however, he can apply it on a much wider scale. The major task of a future revolution, Sternheim writes in 1919, is to cleanse the nation's mentality from a "poisonous ideological tradition"[24] and to initiate the reign of spontaneity, of sensuality, and of aesthetics. If man has, so far, been accustomed to interpret both general history and his own life as a chain of events governed by immutable laws of cause and effect, he should now emphasize his "visionary faculties." He should realize that any given moment is not only a product of earlier events but also contains the seeds of various future developments among which he is free to choose. Similarly, if man has learned to perceive the world through a series of abstract categories, he should now pay attention to the colorful diversity of his surroundings. A society which only teaches its members that pastures are green deprives them of the pleasure which the sight of all the different shades and varieties of grass and herbs can convey to the senses.[25] The emphasis on causality and the predominance of abstract concepts have, in other words, the effect of encaging both man's sensuousness and his imagination. The task of literature, therefore, is "to push open the doors"[26] and to help man regain access to the diversities of the world and of his own character.

Moral and aesthetic encagement or moral and aesthetic anarchy: this is the alternative which Sternheim, in his postwar essays, applies to all the phenomena which he discusses. Yet, in spite of this limitation, his writings can be fascinating for their uncompromising nature and for their perceptual acuity. At the same time, it is their uncompromising individualistic radicalism which has made them almost totally ineffective if not counterproductive. In this regard, Sternheim shares the fate of Ständer, the hero of *Tabula Rasa*. He is unwilling to join any political movement because he is afraid of compromising his tenets for the sake of political effectiveness. Only in individualistic isolation can he remain true to his ideals. At the same time, however, he knows that his individualism will have no general social effect. His prophecies move nobody but the prophet.

Sternheim's novel *Europa*, published in 1919–20, is another clear expression of this dilemma. The novel traces the development of Eura Fuld, a rich heiress, who sacrifices her individuality for the sake of promoting both a sexual and a leftist revolution. In both areas, she cannot help functionalizing the world around her; her social criticism, although valid in itself, operates with systematized evaluative categories; her attitudes toward others are those of a stage director, and her actions, and even her love affairs, are the result of calculations. Only once in her life, at the moment when she leads the revolutionary masses into battle, does she gain a higher freedom, the freedom of ecstasy. This action, however, also results in her death.

Her antagonist, Carl Wundt, is an aesthetic anarchist. A declared foe of both strategies and planning, he attempts to perceive the world around him as if it were made up of animated pictures whose colors and proportions can be savored.[27] This brand of aestheticism results in his total isolation and in his inability to influence, or even to judge, the world around him. Asked about his attitudes vis-à-vis the forthcoming war, he replies:

Curiosity and, beyond that, a peaceful submission, under the robust reality willed by God.

This is cynical, Eura exclaimed.

It definitely allows me the most rewarding, the freest and the most immediate approach, Wundt concluded. (*G*, 5:409)

Wundt's "radicalism," his stance as an increasingly bored spectator who finally retires to a South Pacific island where he can contemplate the immutable azure of the sky, is an expression of aesthetic escapism in its purest form. All in all, the same can be said of Sternheim's own postwar writings. It is not difficult to discern behind the poses of the professed radical the attitudes which had been characteristic of young Sternheim, the aesthete. History still constitutes a power which produces objects of curiosity in ever-new variations. The cult of the Mediterranean or of the South Pacific which occurs in several of his late writings is but a new version of the castle owner's isolationist paradise, and the occasional praise for the self-conscious and self-determined "proletarian" does not do much more than add a new variation to the aesthete's museum of heroic individuals. Sternheim's postwar plays, briefly discussed below, only reaffirm this impression. Their recurrent theme, the victory of uncompromising lovers, is the adequate dramatic image of Sternheim's version of "radical" emancipation. It is, at the same time, a totally private affair. Sternheim's lovers invariably sever their ties to society; they try to operate outside of social relationships. Sternheim's late plays consequently lack almost all the realistic features which had been one of the major qualities of his prewar oeuvre.

The Postwar Plays

Farcical satire, abstract dialogue, and allegorical scenes: these are the major elements which Sternheim combines in most of his postwar dramas. These plays thus carry on the process of dramatic disintegration already observed in an earlier piece, in *1913*, where only those scenes which were of minor thematic importance could be considered genuinely theatrical. In *1913*, Sternheim succeeded in turning Philipp Ernst, the imbecile dandy, into an actor; he could not, however, present the distinctive features of Sofie Maske, the representative of advanced capitalism, in convincing visual terms. Sofie is made an object of abstract discussion and not a subject of self-presentation. Similarly, Sternheim's dramatic technique failed in respect to the two rebel intellectuals of the play, or even worse, his use of theatrical means resulted in an involuntary denunciation of these two figures. Especially Stadler, whom Sternheim intended to present as a positive figure, comes across as nothing more than an inept salesman of hollow ideas. Sternheim obviously tried to counterbalance this effect through the use of allegory in the final scene. Within a basically realistic framework, however, allegory develops counterproductive effects of its own. Stadler's final search for "the great light" did not impress the audience as an expression of utopian hopes. Instead, and understandably, it was interpreted as a further symptom of the empty ideological raptures espoused by this figure.

In Sternheim's postwar dramas this process of disintegration is even more noticeable. From a theatrical point of view, these plays are effective, above all, in their satirical scenes. In Sternheim's works, however, intentional satire is invariably of marginal importance. Theatrical effectiveness thus results in thematic irrelevance. The best example of this dilemma is Sternheim's comedy *The Nebbich*, written and produced in 1922. The petty bourgeois Tritz, to give a brief summary of the plot, is "discovered" by the opera star Rita Marchetti, who introduces him to the glamorous world of postwar society. Tritz, who has the mentality of a sponge, manages to memorize in almost no time the few phrases and slogans which he needs in order to embark on a successful career in such fields as diplomacy, art criticism, or political journalism. He is nothing but the echo of his protectress Rita, and he delivers his speeches in the manner of a parrot. Sternheim could unquestionably make full use of his theatrical experience in devising this figure, and many of the scenes in which Tritz is shown are quite effective. The jokes of the play are, however, easy jokes; they rely on the widely shared notion that diplomats are zombies and journalists babblers.

The Nebbich also fails for a second reason. Once again, Sternheim explores the theme of the social climber; in contrast to *Paul Schippel Esq.* and *The Snob*, however, he presents not his success but his ultimate failure. Both Rita's sexual demands and the public's intellectual expectations are more than Tritz's body can take, and the petty bourgeois is thus happy to return to his former surroundings. Cobbler stick to your last: this had already been Theobald Maske's device for his own life. Yet in *The Bloomers*, this sentence resulted, if, not from emancipatory, then at least from provocative intentions. In *The Nebbich*, the same message is no more than an indication of haughty snobbishness; the play does indeed deliver the message which Sternheim's critics had mistakenly read into his earlier plays: the contempt of the philistine.[28]

As is amply demonstrated by *The Nebbich*, Sternheim had abandoned his original hopes that the middle class might rediscover their original character; he had concluded instead that they were hopelessly corrupted and unsuitable for dramatic presentation. This conclusion did not, however, result in attempts to replace the heroic bourgeois by the self-conscious and self-determined worker. *Tabula Rasa*, the play in which Sternheim had made such an attempt, remained without a successor. Instead, the author chose to follow the line which he had started at the end of 1913. With the exception of Tritz, the heroes of his late plays are "radical" intellectuals and as such they share Stadler's major characteristics. They indulge in highly abstract discussions and when they act, they do so in theatrically unconvincing, quasi-allegorical scenes.

Allegory and discussions are indeed the only technical devices used in Sternheim's first postwar play, *The Unchained Contemporary*. The drama presents Klara, a rich heiress and the symbolic representative of "Germany's young girls," surrounded by a diplomat, an admiral, an opera tenor, a journalist, and a politician. These men are conceived as the most advanced prototypes of the European male, and Klara is to choose one of them as her husband. Along comes Klette, the "unchained contemporary," and carries away the prize. Where the others, who consider themselves mere functions of universal rational systems, devise strategies and calculate, Klette preaches the gospel of complete spontaneity and abhors any categories which tie together the individual and his social surroundings or even the dimensions of time—the past, the present, and the future. He preaches, and his author has obvious difficulties in translating his sermons into drama. The climactic point of the action, to give but one example, reads like this: the group goes sailing, Klara falls into the water, and Klette is the only one who tries to save her although he does not even know how to swim. Klette's action stands in the tradition of the heroic fool[29] who refuses to let his actions be governed by petty calculations. Yet all this happens offstage: it is not shown, but simply made the subject of discussion and narration.

The Fossil, the play following *The Nebbich*, can be considered slightly more successful in this respect. The action takes place in a half-allegorical, half-realistic scenery, in the estate of Traugott Beeskow, a retired Prussian general and the father-in-law of Sofie Maske. Following the war and the revolution, Beeskow has severed all ties to society and spends his days in the astrological observatory which he has installed in his castle. His daughter Ursula, meanwhile, works in a chemical laboratory in the basement. Both Beeskow and his daughter are, according to Sternheim's rather private allegorical semantics, true aristocrats in that they are concerned only with the immutable substance of things.

TRAUGOTT: What's water?
URSULA: H_2O.

TRAUGOTT: Exactly! The fact that it can be made into mineral water is completely irrelevant. Pure accident.

URSULA: Beeskow for ever! (*R*, 251; *G*, 1:302)[30]

Traugott's son Otto, the husband of Sofie Maske and thus an aristocratic apostate, shares Ursula's laboratory. His middle-class mentality has given him a taste for technical experiments. Within the thematic confrontation of the play, however, he does not count any more. "The middle classes, upper or lower" are "colorless characters," "they are a boom and burst bunch, a miserable lot" (*R*, 254; *G*, 1:307) who would be willing to accept anybody and anything—even Communism. They have thus ceased to play a historical role. The aristocracy, on the other hand, is still a power to be counted upon: "even in present-day Germany it's still productive."

Beeskow's antagonist is Ago von Bohna, a former aristocrat, who has been converted to leftist teachings. On his return from Moscow, he makes a stopover in Traugott's house and thus arouses the retired general from his lethargy. Beeskow, who has again found an adversary worthy of being fought, sends his daughter into the forefront with the mission to sound out the enemy. After some initial theoretical discussions, Ago and Ursula fall in love with each other, whereupon Traugott shoots and kills them both. For the ending of the play Sternheim wrote two different versions. The first one emphasizes the revolutionary determination of Traugott's chauffeur Otto Föhrkolb, a member of the Communist party. To make sure that Traugott will not escape justice, Föhrkolb pulls out his revolver and, pointing at him, says: "No one touches him! This time we'll carry through all the way" (*G*, 1:580). The second, that is, the published, version emphasizes the triumph of the murderer and the servility of the "proletarian." Traugott is advised to flee across the border but he prefers to be driven to police headquarters:

What can happen to me in this day and age? Eh, you idiot?! Eh? (And when Otto, rigidly, does not answer, Traugott goes on forcefully.) Well, then! (Then to Föhrkolb in a rasping voice of command.) Forward— quick—march! Above all, there must be order and justice in Germany! Hurrah! (And goes out erect and bareheaded, dragging the chauffeur after him.) (*R*, 285; *G*, 1:359)

The victory of the determined proletarian revolutionary or the cynical triumph of reactionary forces: these are the two historical possibilities hinted at in these two endings. The play can, from this aspect and especially with the final version, be read as an accurate and bitter analysis of the political conditions of the Weimar Republic and as an anticipation of the Hitler years. It is not surprising, therefore, that Franz Pfemfert consented to printing the play in his journal *Die Aktion*, and that the book edition of the drama was illustrated by George Grosz, one of the most politically active German artists of the twenties. A careful reading of the text, however, makes it difficult to sustain such an unequivocal political interpretation, and the final scene already gives sufficient grounds for suspicion. The general, it is true, resorts to murder, and his question, "What can happen to me in this day and age?" is a bitter comment on the partiality of the German judicial system at a time. when judges were generally loath to punish right-wing political criminals. At the same time, however, Sternheim does not hide his admiration for the general who leaves the scene "erect and bareheaded," with the dignity of a soldier who has done his duty, "dragging the chauffeur behind him."

The aesthete and the political thinker, one might conclude from such observations, are once more at odds with each other, and the final scene, while ostensibly denouncing the victory of reactionary forces in postwar Germany, also helps to reconfirm the earlier statement that the aristocracy is still "a productive force," even in its fossil stage. This belief in the continuing productivity of the feudal relics of society is central to the play from a different aspect as well. It is true that Sternheim treats Ago von Bohna, Beeskow's leftist opponent, with respect, and that he uses him, to a certain extent, as the spokesman of his own ideas. When questioned by Ursula, Ago explains his political creed in the following terms:

We stop a long way short of Marx, but go beyond Bakunin in demanding both religion and art. Proletarian, of course! Dreams and, where appropriate, utter madness. We are less inhibited than you are, unbiased; but we want all this not as something private, we want it to spring from the common purpose of federalistically minded human beings. (*R*, 280; *G*, 1:353)

Ago, in other words, is anything but a Marxian Socialist; rather he is a representative of the anarchist currents of thought as they were dominant in Franz Pfemfert's *Aktion*. In the course of the play, however, or, more precisely, in the course of his love affair with Ursula, Ago is led to give up the only genuinely political element of his thinking, the propagation of the "federalistically minded human being." According to his initial thoughts, the insistence on privacy, that is, on the privacy of love, is a relic of feudal times; it is a notion which the young generation has to overcome. Lovemaking, he argues, is a social affair since it produces a third human being, the child.

> AGO: The significance of the sexual act lies not in the sexual pleasure of the male or the female, but in the fate of the child.
> URSULA: It's significance lies in the sweet release it offers from all restrictions.
> AGO: Such anarchy is called feudalism. Après nous le déluge.
> URSULA: Long live the sexual impluse!
> AGO: You, a lady of the ancient aristocracy, shout that in 1923.
> URSULA: Aristocracy is still productive! (*R*, 271; *G*, 1:336)

"Feudal," that is, individualistic, anarchism on the one hand, social "federalistic" anarchism on the other: this is the central thematic antithesis of the play and one of Sternheim's major subjects of debate in the postwar years. The collisons between Ständer and Sturm in *Tabula Rasa*, between Klara and Klette in *The Unchained Contemporary*, between Eura and Carl Wundt in the novel *Europa*: all these debates revolve around the same question. More than that, the glorification of totally asocial actions as the epitome of human freedom can be considered the one central theme in Sternheim's works in general. Don Juan's wish of "holding, for one starlit night, his mother in his arms like a sweet woman"[31] is thus an early anticipation of Ursula's praise of the "sweet release" which love offers "from all restrictions." In all these cases, Sternheim sides with the anarchical lovers and against the anarchistic politicians. In *The Fossil*, the radical Ago von Bohna is thus driven to throw his manuscript, the fruit of long years of political thinking, into the fire: he realizes that he cannot reconcile his experience of love with his "federalistic" denunciation of privacy and spontaneity.

Uznach School: Culture Criticism and Nostalgia

The year in which *The Fossil* was published, 1923, marked the end of the precarious initial period of the Weimar Republic. The following five years were characterized by relative social and political stability; they were, in other words, not a fertile time for exercises in political radicalism or for the staging of political plays. It is, therefore, no coincidence that *The Fossil* was Sternheim's last attempt at political drama and that his next play, *Oscar Wilde*, bears the signs of a partial retreat. It presents the anti-authoritarian individual in the guise of the dandy and thus indicates the author's open return to tenets which he had held in his earliest years. Understandably, the publication of *Oscar Wilde* resulted in a definitive break with the Aktionskreis, which expected its members to take a directly political stand, and with such moderate critics as Kurt Pinthus, who until then had still hoped that Sternheim might some day find his way back to his "calling": the writing of middle-class satires.

While Sternheim did nothing to comply with such expectations, he seems to have noticed that the dramatic presentation of dandyish heroes or, for that matter, of great lovers of past ages, led only to a dead end. In 1925, he started working on a new project which resulted in the publication of *Lutetia*, *Reports on European Politics*, and *Arts and National Life*. Obviously inspired by Heinrich Heine's travel books, *Lutetia* exemplifies Sternheim's determination to come to terms with the "spirit" of the twenties. *Uznach School*, the play which was published in the following year, is a similar example of Sternheim's renewed interest in "contemporary" questions. Both the subtitle of the play, "Neue Sachlichkeit" [New Objectivity], and its major theme, the changing relationships between the sexes, are reflections on central ideological and cultural trends of the time.

The travel book *Lutetia* as well as the play *Uznach School* indicate Sternheim's awareness that the postwar period had effected profound changes not only in European politics but also in all areas of cultural life—changes which needed reporting, comparing, and evaluating. Women were gaining new freedoms; taboos concerning sexuality and the presentation of the human body were being disregarded; sexual role stereotypes were in a state of change and, more so than in the prewar years, the amusement districts of the big cities took on the appearance of a perpetual carnival. Most important perhaps, many of the cherished ideals and ideologies of the middle classes were falling into disrepute. It was becoming fashionable to show a certain air of cynicism and detached "objectivity" vis-à-vis that which had once been considered "higher values."

For Sternheim, such changes were a source of both fascination and irritation. He had always demanded that a writer be guided by an "enthusiasm for reality" and that he capture and present the essence of his historical period. More important yet, many of the characteristic developments of those roaring years were peculiarly related to his own previous writings. They could easily appear as belated realizations of Sternheim's prewar messages, and it is indeed quite likely that his comedies, had they been written in the twenties, would have found a different reception and a public willing to appreciate, if not their message, then at least their ambivalence and their irony. Theobald Maske's contempt of cultural values, Christian's rational attitude toward the most sacred familial bonds, the spirit of the machine age which permeates Sternheim's novellas: all these could easily have sailed under the now popular flag of "new objectivity."[32]

And yet, it seems to have been just this very resemblance between his earlier demands and their apparent realizations which confronted the author with a particular dilemma and which prevented him from showing any "enthusiasm for reality." Sternheim's concept of emancipation had rested on the assumption that each individual should follow his own drives. The postwar displays of freedom and joy were, by contrast, produced by the laws of the market and staged by the culture industries. Rather than being a genuine expression of individual desires, they amounted to a set of social demands, to new sources of exertion and struggle. "Look how mother and child are sweating," Sternheim's early dramatic hero Don Juan had said in order to characterize his contemporaries' efforts at displaying their heroic character.[33] The heroine of Sternheim's last play, *Uznach School*, makes the very same remark (*G*, 3:409). In contrast to her predecessor, however, she is confronted not with would-be heroes willing to sacrifice themselves for some general good, but—and this is an even more problematic phenomenon—with a group of young girls exerting themselves in the enactment of their own freedom.[34]

The scene of the play is an upper-class boarding school for girls whose director, Siebenstern, advocates avant garde principles in pedagogy as well as in all other aspects of life. His major educational goal is to make his students "truly contemporary," to teach them to stand in the forefront of cultural developments. The end of the war has produced radical changes in the roles and the self-understanding of the sexes, and a postwar woman should, therefore, break with all traditional role stereotypes. The loss of virginity is considered an implicit entrance requirement for the school; it is the first step in an educational program which aims at abolishing all inhibitions relating to the body, to sexuality, and to the expression of emotions and desires.

The play leaves no doubt that Siebenstern's pedagogical principles are part of a potentially positive cultural tendency. His explicit goal is to help his students to establish their own personality, a goal which is certainly in agreement with the theatrical message which Sternheim had propagated throughout his life. And yet these laudable efforts have not produced positive results. On the contrary, Siebenstern's pupils are not free human beings. Instead, they remain pawns in an educational program and—what is worse—they are the slaves of their own emancipatory rhetoric.

In the first act, Sternheim chooses the realm of verbal communication in order to demonstrate this peculiar dialectic. The girls meet for one of their daily encounter sessions with the headmaster. Siebenstern acts *in loco parentis*; his authority, however, is minimal. The girls have broken the chains of cultural traditions, of parental authority and male dominance, and they see no reason why they should submit to a school director. For all this, however, power structures are still manifest; they have only taken on a new form. In their constant efforts to display their freedom, the girls unconsciously submit to their own dogmatism and to its major agent, the peer group. It is the general expectation that each member of the group is willing, at any given moment, to verbalize her feelings and to express her most hidden thoughts. The demonstration of freedom thus turns into a new competitive game to be played under the ever watchful eye of a newly established authority whose power is even more redoutable since it leaves the individual no possibilities of retreat. To comply with the norms of the group means to renounce even those niches of privacy which had, in earlier times, offered the individual a chance of enjoying at least a minimal amount of liberty.

In the second act, the same mechanism is presented again, although from a different aspect. Clothed in bathing suits and thus exhibiting the privacy of their bodies, the girls are shown in one of the gymnastics lessons which constitute a major part of the school's program. Here again, every moment is accompanied by verbal statements explaining the physical functions and the emotional effect of each part of the exercises. As it turns out in these statements, the girls have succeeded in internalizing the teachings of the "new objectivity" movement. They experience their own bodies in the form of machines in which each muscle and each limb is given a specific task which it has to fulfill for the sake of the entire system.

The process of calculated rationalization does not, however, stop at this point. The body machines, which are trained in these lessons, are not ends in themselves, but rather elements within a larger system of social relationships. They are tools of self advertising, and thus instruments of power. Sternheim emphasizes this additional and—to him—central aspect by turning the school lawn, the practicing ground for the gym lessons, into a stage and by presenting the students as if they were members of a burlesque show, one of the major theatrical discoveries of that decade. In displaying their own emancipation and their physical competence, the girls also enact their own commercials: they demonstrate the control which they have over their own bodies, the power which they wield as a group, and they advertise themselves as sources of irresistible pleasure.

Like all theatrical representations which are part of a power structure, such enactments require the presence of spectators. Within the play, this role is assumed by two additional characters: by Mathilde, a girl who has grown up in the provincial town of Lüneburg, and by Siebenstern's son Klaus, who has just returned from a trip around the world. One of the functions of the girls' self-presentations is to impress and to initiate the outsider, in this case Mathilde, who is to become a member of the group. As it turns out, she is ill suited for the school's program. She is sexually inexperienced and, above all, she does not understand why she should be "sweating" in order to be free. The second target of the performance is equally hard to win over. Obviously, a display of female charms aims at impressing the male. The gym lessons are thus only the beginning of a sequence which culminates in a later scene in which two of the girls invade the privacy of Klaus's room. This particular male, however, refuses to act within a scenario which has been written for him and which he considers undramatic, mechanical, and boring.

Against this mechanization of sexuality, Klaus holds up the old script of seduction: the moon-lit nights, the dark cloaks, the ladders and daggers. Confronted with the equivalent of burlesque shows, he dreams of the delights of a nineteenth-century city rambler rapturing at the sight of a woman's leg unexpectedly and furtively exposed by the blowing wind. Pushed into the role of a modern day Paris and made to choose among the girls, Klaus opts for the girl from Lüneburg and her old-fashioned provincial charm.[35]

Obviously, the author of the play supports this option. The school, it turns out, will have to close; most of the girls prefer to leave an institution in which Klaus, the romantic dreamer, and Mathilde, the relic of a provincial past, set the example. Their flight, however, only emphasizes the triumph of these two new model heroes. The last scene presents them as cultural idols: in the pose of Fra Angelico's angels, holding their fingers to their lips, they silently ascend the stairs while the orchestra intones one of Boccherini's minuets.

From a theatrical point of view, *Uznach School* is certainly the most convincing example of Sternheim's postwar plays. In his other late dramas, the author had obvious difficulties in translating his concepts into dramatic pictures; in this comedy, he makes full use of the images and scenic arrangements produced by the culture and fashion industry of the twenties. The glamor girls of the news and fashion magazines, the presentational techniques developed in the modern dance movement and in athletics, the uniforms devised for motor cyclists, dancers, and swimmers, the exhibitionist rituals developed by the peer groups of the young generation in both Europe and the United States: all these and other pictorial arrangements are effectively integrated into the play. Once again the theme is in agreement with the medium, and the roles of theater are part of the play's thematic texture.

In spite of such achievements, however, *Uznach School* can hardly be read or seen without some misgivings. These are aroused not by the critical stance of the play, but the author's additional attempts at solving the dilemma which he presents and by his efforts to convey a positive message to his spectators. In other words, *Uznach School*, like many of Sternheim's works, raises doubts at the moment when the author exchanges the role of the critic for that of a teacher.

Why have Siebenstern's efforts or—more generally speaking—why have the cultural changes of the twenties not produced the freedom which they had promised? One of Sternheim's answers is that they were not sufficiently radical. As Siebenstern's son Klaus puts it, the school still operates within the narrow tracks of Western civilization and it still reproduces civilization's most characteristic evils: the will to power and the obsession with rational calculation. In opposition to such limitations, Klaus indulges in myths of precivilized freedom and thus elaborates on a theme which frequently occurs in Sternheim's works. In *Don Juan*, Sternheim had propagated the freedom of Oedipus; in his novellas he had extolled the ecstasies of the insane; in his essays he had spoken of the pleasures of Dionysian life. Klaus, in reference to Gottfried Benn, praises those "whole nations which lie in the sand and blow into bamboo reeds."[36]

Uznach School is dedicated to Gottfried Benn and the above quotation is certainly central to Benn's thinking. It is also in at least partial agreement with the spirit of Sternheim's prewar comedies. To spend one's life "lying in the sand": this regressive fantasy is not a realistic remedy for the evils of civilization; it is, however, literarily effective as a contrastive image and as a provocative stimulus of thought. Sternheim's glorification of the philistine and of the social climber, his presentation of comic heroes obsessed with keeping alive the "moribund" qualities of the human character, had been effective in the very same manner. It was a further advantage of these figures that they were also realistically plausible. Being constructed from the very material which was characteristic also for the society which Sternheim attacked, being both typically middle class and strikingly theatrical, these figures could be considered the real finds of an obsessed collector.

The ending of *Uznach School* and for that matter the end of Sternheim's dramatic oeuvre is void of these qualities. Rather than relying on his aggressive fantasies, the playwright contents himself with a nostalgic citation of familiar cultural images: he cites a scene from one of Victor Hugo's novels, an early Renaissance painting, a late eighteenth-century minuet and the charm of Lüneburg and the German provincial past. Such citations are relatively moderate. They may even be said to offer a more humane model of life than could be found in any of Sternheim's earlier plays. For this reason, they seem to be less convincing.

Notes and References

Preface

1. Cf. Rudolf Billetta, *Sternheim-Kompendium* (Wiesbaden, 1975). Billetta gives a complete account of the editions, translations, and performances of Sternheim's works and of the journalistic and scholarly writings on the author.

2. Sternheim's play *Die Hose* was staged twice in England: in 1963 in London under the title *The Knickers* and in 1970 in Brighton under the title *The Bloomers*.

3. Cf. the statistics given by Wolfgang Herles, "Die Sternheim-Renaissance auf den deutschen Bühnen der Bundesrepublik," in *Carl Sternheim's Dramen*, ed. Jörg Schönert (Heidelberg, 1975), p. 207–22.

4. Gottfried Friedrich Wilhelm Hegel, *Ästhetik*, ed. F. Bassenge (Frankfurt: Europäische Verlagsanstalt, 1955), 2:571.

5. This interpretation has been given by critics such as Paul Rilla, *Essays* (Berlin: Henschel, 1955), pp. 202–09 or Hellmuth Karasek, *Sternheim* (Velber, 1965) and in practically all works dealing with Sternheim in the context of early twentieth-century German drama.

6. For this type of interpretation cf. Wolfgang Wendler, *Carl Sternheim: Weltvorstellung und Kunstprinzipien* (Frankfurt, 1966) and Wilhelm Emrich, "Carl Sternheim's 'Kampf der Metapher,' " in his *Geist und Widergeist* (Frankfurt: Athenäum, (1965), pp. 163–84.

7. Cf. Hans-Lothar Peter, *Literarische Intelligenz und Klassenkampf: Die Aktion 1911–1932* (Cologne, 1972).

8. An attempt to explain Sternheim's work as an expression of "Wilhelminian" neuroticism has been made by Winfried G. Sebald, *Carl Sternheim: Kritiker und Opfer der Wilhelminischen Ära* (Stuttgart, 1969).

Chapter One

1. It is customary among literary historians to consider Sternheim part of the expressionist movement. Such a grouping ignores the fact that Sternheim belongs to an earlier group of writers than most expressionists, that he wrote his major works before the beginning of World War I, and that he retained a critical attitude toward expressionism. It is, therefore, no coinci-

dence that the emphasis on the "expressionist" aspects of his works has contributed little to the understanding of their central intentions and stylistic features. Cf. Wolfgang Paulsen, "Carl Sternheim und die Komödie des Expressionismus," in *Die deutsche Komödie im* 20. *Jahrhundert*, ed. Wolfgang Paulsen (Heidelberg, 1976), p. 95, and Hans Kaufmann, *Krisen und Wandlungen der deutschen Literatur von Wedekind bis Feuchtwanger* (Berlin: Aufbau, 1969), p. 300.

2. Quotations from Sternheim's works are based on Carl Sternheim, *Gesamtwerk*, ed. Wilhelm Emrich, 10 vol. (Neuwied, 1961–76), cited in the text as *G*. The translations are mine unless otherwise indicated.

3. Several passages in Sternheim's works and letters indicate that his admiration for his father, as expressed in the autobiography, was largely fictitious. Young Sternheim seems to have viewed his father with a good deal of contempt and embarrassment. Cf. Irmtraut Haimerl, "Zwischen Antisemitismus und Akkulturation," in *Carl Sternheim's Dramen*, pp. 137–52, and Manfred Linke, *Carl Sternheim* (Reinbek, 1979), pp. 9–12.

4. The importance of this biographical fact is stressed by Wolfgang Paulsen (*Die deutsche Komödie*, p. 100), who points out that Sternheim's plays are a unique example of "Berlinian" comedies.

5. Cf. Sternheim, *Gesamtwerk*, vol. 10, pt. 1, pp. 195–97.

6. Similar characterizations of prewar German society are found in Sternheim's drama *1913*, in his novel *Europa*, and in his essay *Berlin or Juste Milieu*.

7. Perhaps the most striking parallel to Sternheim's version of this aestheticist question and to his attempts at answering it can be found in Hugo von Hofmannsthal's "Briefe des Zurückgekehrten," in *Gesammelte Werke, Prosa* (Frankfurt: S. Fischer, 1959), 2:279–310. Hofmannsthal quotes Addison's demand that "the whole man must move at once" and measures his contemporaries with the yardstick of this ideal. The consequences to which the application of this principle leads are just as gruesome as they sometimes are in Sternheim's work. Hofmannsthal, in these letters, prefers uninhibited cruelty and ruthlessness to the ambivalent attitudes and moral qualms exhibited by modern man.

8. For the political and cultural importance of such idols cf. Bill Kinser and Neil Kleinman, *The Dream that Was no More a Dream. A Search for Esthetic Reality in Germany 1890–1945*. (New York: Harper and Row, 1969).

9. This is true in spite of the correct observation that some of Sternheim's early works, especially his poetry, show traces of Stefan George's style. Cf. Manfred Durzak, *Stefan George* (Stuttgart: Kohlhammer, 1974), pp. 123–26.

10. The same can be said for Sternheim's comedies and novellas, which demonstrate the possibility given any individual to realize his own character even under the adverse conditions of modern society. The literary character is thus, according to Sternheim's intentions, a model to be emulated by the audience.

11. This ambivalence is caused not by the author's shortsightedness but by an objective dilemma which can be explained in the following terms. Jost Hermand ("Gründerzeit und bürgerlicher Realismus," in *Monatshefte* 59, no. 3 (1967):106–17) has plausibly argued that, from 1870 on, the aesthetic ideal of the great, heroic personality was propagated by the German bourgeoisie. Sternheim's call for the strong middle-class hero can thus be interpreted as an offshoot of this ideological tradition. On the other hand, Sternheim was aware of the fact that twentieth-century societies tend to eliminate the dramatic and presentational elements of human behavior. Placed within this broader historical context, his works are an expression not of bourgeois ideology but of aesthetic opposition.

12. This specific problem of the dandy is discussed by Otto Mann, *Der Dandy*, 2d ed. (Heidelberg, 1962). For a discussion of Sternheim's dandyism cf. Peter Uwe Hohendahl, *Das Bild der bürgerlichen Welt im expressionistischen Drama* (Heidelberg: Winter, 1967), p. 67.

13. Franz Blei, *Erzählung eines Lebens* (Leipzig: Paul List, 1930), p. 434.

14. As, for instance, in the early drama "Erlösung" (1899), in *Gesamtwerk*, 8:239–66.

15. Cf. "Brüder," in *Gesamtwerk*, 9:251, 573.

16. "Ich bin der Herr dein Gott," in *Gesamtwerk*, 8:664.

17. *Ibid.*, 8:664.

18. *Ibid.*, 7:51.

19. Cf. *ibid.*, vol. 10, pt. 2, p. 1130.

20. Many of these thoughts show the influence of Friedrich Nietzsche and of the Neo-Kantian philosopher Ernst Rickert. Sternheim's indebtedness to Rickert has been demonstrated by Wendler, *Sternheim* pp. 230–39; for Nietzsche's influence on Sternheim cf. Herbert W. Reichert, "Nietzsche und Carl Sternheim," in *Nietzsche und die deutsche Literatur*, ed. Bruno Hillebrand (Tübingen, 1978), 2:11–34.

21. Cf. Walter H. Sokel, *The Writer in Extremis* (New York, 1964), pp. 55–118.

22. For this aspect cf. above all Sternheim's novella "Der Anschluss," in *Gesamtwerk*, 4:267–96.

23. Cf. Wendler, *Sternheim*, p. 245.

24. "Ich bin der Herr dein Gott" (*Gesamtwerk*, 8:667–68).

25. "Bei sengender Glut finden unter dem Himmel von Arles und

Auvers in Busch und Kornfeldern Mysterien eines Liebestraumels statt zwischen aufgespreizter Natur und einem Mann, der ihr Inneres durchwühlend die Trophäen ihrer Eingeweide als Überwinder aufzeigend zum Himmel hebt!" (*Gestamtwerk*, 6:12).

26. "Das Drama liegt in der überwältigenden Macht der *Persönlichkeit*, die den *Künstler* vergewaltigte."

27. An interpretation of the general psychological and political significance of such images in early twenthieth-century perception is given by Klaus Theweleit, *Männerphantasien* (Frankfurt: Roter Stern, 1977).

28. For an attempt to interpret Sternheim's work within the context of phenomenology cf. Winfried Freund, *Die Bürgerkomödien Carl Sternheims* (Munich: Fink, 1976).

29. Friedrich Nietzsche, *Werke*, ed. Karl Schlechta (Munich: Hanser, 1954), 1:34.

30. Cf., for instance, Silvio Vietta and Hans Georg Kemper, *Expressionismus* (Munich, 1975), p. 101.

31. This is the premise and conclusion of the study by Sebald.

32. Marianne Kesting, "Zweifel und Carl Sternheim," in her *Auf der Suche nach der Realität. Kritische Schriften zur modernen Literatur* (Munich: R. Piper, 1972), p. 201.

33. For a discussion of this term, which is central to Sternheim's thinking, cf. Wendler, *Sternheim*, pp. 119–30 and Sebald, *Sternheim*, pp. 38–46.

34. "Von den paar hundert Prominenten auf allen Gebieten, die wir als Gäste bei uns gesehen hatten, war kaum ein halbes Dutzend imstande gewesen, uns wenigstens soweit, dass der Begriff des Einzelnen feststand, zu bereichern."

35. Cf. *Gesamtwerk*, vol. 10, pt. 1, p. 268, where Sternheim gives examples of such raw material, i.e., of acquaintances who served as models for his literary characters.

36. To contribute to a "redramatization" of social life through a redramatization of the stage can be considered one of the central intentions of Sternheim's oeuvre from his earliest dramatic attempts up to his late works in the twenties. To ascribe primarily "artistic" and "theatrical" intentions to his plays as is done by Horst Denkler, *Das Drama des Expressionismus* (Munich, 1967), p. 76, results in reductive interpretations.

37. The play was first published in the highly regarded journal *Hyperion* and appeared under the protection and with the blessings of Franz Blei, one of Sternheim's friends and, at the same time, one of the most prolific literary impresarios and "discoverers" of the prewar period.

Chapter Two

1. For Sternheim's attempts to find a composer for his play cf. *Gesamtwerk*, vol. 10, pt. 2, p. 1146.

2. Cervantes is one of the characters of the play. He hears Don Juan express his beliefs and thus presumably conceives the idea for writing his novel *Don Quixote*.

3. Cf. Hermann Broch, "Das Böse im Wertsystem der Kunst," in his *Gesammelte Werke, Essays*, ed. Hannah Ahrendt (Zürich: Rhein-Verlag, 1955), 1:311–50.

4. Don Juan's relationship to his fellow human beings, as expressed in this scene, is central to Sternheim's own concept of social relationships and thus deserves to be quoted at some length:

> Am Nächsten reizt mich nur des köstlich Eigene,
> Nichtzuerratende an Weg und Ziel.
> Je stolzer er in dunklem Mantel geht,
> schlägt um so rasender in mir Begierde,
> um seinen Glauben, seine letzte Sehnsucht
> zu wissen, und in tiefster Brust zu prüfen,
> ob nicht mein eigenes Herz noch höher zuckt.
>
> *(Gesamtwerk*, 7:690)

5. Many of Sternheim's later works still express similar anarchic desires. They differ from *Don Juan*, however, by taking into consideration the specific historical and social conditions of man's psyche.

6. The belief that the feudal anarchism of the Middle Ages offered one last opportunity for the development—and hence for the literary depiction —of heroic characters is central to the literary theories of German classicism. Cf. Hegel, *Ästhetik*, 2:463–66.

7. In his later references to *Don Juan*, Sternheim considered this scene central to the meaning of the play. Cf. *Gesamtwerk*, 6:93, 218, 311.

8. In his later writings, Sternheim vehemently attacked what he considered a functionalization of love in more explicit terms. Cf. chapter 9 of this study. For an extensive discussion of the Oedipal theme in Sternheim's works cf. Wolfgang Wendler, "Sternheims Wirklichkeit," in *Carl Sternheim*, ed. W. Wendler (Darmstadt, 1980).

9. Cf., above all, his Molière essay written in 1917 *(Gesamtwerk*, 6:17).

10. Cf. "Tasso oder Kunst des Juste Milieu," *Gesamtwerk*, 6:196–98.

Chapter Three

1. The German title of the play is *Die Hose*. The quotations from the text are taken from *The Bloomers*, trans. M. A. McHaffie, in *Scenes from the Heroic Life of the Middle Classes* by Carl Sternheim, ed. J. M. Ritchie (London, 1970), hereafter cited in the text as *R*.

2. The denunciation of the "philistine," i.e., of the limited horizon of the petit bourgeois, is one of the recurrent themes of German literature between romanticism and expressionism. Cf. Hohendahl, pp. 100–113.

3. For the relationship between Sternheim and his public see my "Aufklärungskomödien im 'Massenzeitalter': Über Carl Sternheims Beziehungen zum Publikum," *Jahrbuch der deutschen Schillergesellschaft* 19 (1975): 284–305.

4. *Gesamtwerk*, 6:7.

5. Siegfried Jacobsohn in *Das Jahr der Bühne* 2 (1912–13): 151.

6. Cf. a similar use of the "cloak metaphor" in Sternheim's *Don Juan* (*Gesamtwerk*, 7:690).

7. Like most contemporaries, Sternheim interpreted Nietzsche's will to power in a Darwinian sense, i.e., as a concept of objective historical or biological development. The will to power is the major element in Nietzsche's writings which he criticized throughout his work. Cf. *Gesamtwerk*, 5:343, 6:453, 7:686.

8. This fact can help to explain the unique and bewildering identity of comic and—in a "bourgeois" sense—heroic features in Sternheim's plays. As a typical figure of comedy, Maske reduces sublime values to their most material meaning. In doing so, however, he embraces a mode of perception which, according to Sternheim, is characteristic of the bourgeois and certainly typical of the objective status of ideals in capitalist societies. For this interpretation of Sternheim's works see Ludwig Marcuse, "Das expressionistische Drama," in *Literaturgeschichte der Gegenwart*, ed. L. Marcuse (Leipzig, 1925), 2:149.

9. Cf. Siegfried Jacobsohn in *Die Schaubühne* 7 (1911): 202, and Hans Schwerte, "Carl Sternheim: *Die Hose*," *Der Deutschunterricht* 15, no.6 (1963): 59–80.

10. For Sternheim's demand that the "ordinary" be the subject matter of literature cf. *Gesamtwerk* 6:25, 45, and chapter 6 of this study.

11. A different interpretation is given by Durzak (*Expressionistisches Drama*, p. 67), who assumes that Maske sees through his renters' intentions from the very start.

12. Cf. Jürgen Habermas, *Strukturwandel der Öffentlichkeit* (Neuwied: Luchterhand, 1962), pp. 60–75.

13. The subtitle of the play is "Ein bürgerliches Lustspiel," which obviously refers to the eighteenth-century genre of "bürgerliches Trauerspiel." In this context, the term "bürgerlich" can have the meaning "bourgeois," "middle class," or "domestic."

Chapter Four

1. The German title of the play is *Die Kassette*. Quotations from the text are taken from *The Strongbox*, trans. Maurice Edwards and Valerie Reich, in *Anthology of German Expressionist Drama*, ed. Walter Sokel (New York, 1963), pp. 90–157, hereafter cited as *S*. Emendations of the text of this translation were necessary at some points.

2. This is a common cause for misinterpretations of the play. Most critics tend to follow Paul Rilla's (*Essays*, pp. 202–9) dictum that Krull, in the course of the play, is deprived of both his sensual pleasure and his peace of mind. Krull, on the other hand, states that the strongbox offers more sensual pleasure to him than his wife who has unveiled all her secrets and thus lost her charm.

3. Called "Lurley" in the original, a term which emphasizes Krull's "medieval" fantasies. Cf. also the interpretation of this scene given by Winfried Freund, *Bürgerkomödien*, p. 39.

4. Cf. Kinser and Kleinman, *Dream*.

5. There is, as far as I can see, only one scene in the play in which the buying power of money is mentioned.

6. The original says: "Sinnbild hergebrachten Bürgerwohlstandes."

7. To have missed this point is the basic shortcoming in the interpretation of the *Strongbox* given by Hans-Peter Bayerdörfer, "Non olet—altes Thema und neues Sujet," *Euphorion* 67 (1973): 323–58.

8. The German text emphasizes the difference between "Eigentum" and "Besitz." For the same thought, cf. *The Snob* (*Gesamtwerk*, 1:170), where Sternheim distinguishes between "erborgt" and "ersessen."

9. According to Sternheim's later works, the difference between the feudal and middle class notion of ownership coincides with different concepts of the ego and of the substance of things. The nobility emphasizes the immutable character of all objects, the middle class their changeability, and the various possible relationships between them. Cf. *Gesamtwerk*, 1:302, 317; 6:242–43.

10. A similar notion is central to Sternheim's drama *1913*.

11. It is interesting to note that none of the interpretations of *The Strongbox* which I have seen pays any attention to this learning process. Instead, critics insist on the notion that this comedy knows "no action and

no development" (Helmut Arntzen, "Die unmenschliche Komödie," in his *Literatur im Zeitalter der Information* [Frankfurt: Athenäum, 1971], 301–4), or they even argue that the last two acts of the play are relatively weak and do not offer any new aspects (Bernhard Diebold, *Anarchie im Drama*, 4th ed. [Berlin: H. Keller, 1928], p. 95). Hans-Peter Bayerdörfer ("Sternheim: *Die Kassette*," in *Die deutsche Komödie vom Mittelalter bis zur Gegenwart*, ed. Walter Hinck [Düsseldorf, 1977], pp. 213–32) tries to give the play a more profound meaning by presenting Krull as a quasi-tragic figure and by interpreting Sternheim's comedies in the light of the melancholic concept of the genre which had been prevalent in *fin-de-siècle* literature. Most blatant perhaps is Durzak's interpretation of the play's ending. Durzak (*Expressionistisches Drama*, 1:84) succeeds in presenting Krull as the perpetual fool and loser by ascribing to him the final words of the play, words which are in fact uttered by Seidenschnur.

    12. Cf. Karasek, p. 57.

Chapter Five

    1. The German title is *Bürger Schippel*. Quotations are taken from *Paul Schippel Esq.*, trans. M. A. L. Brown, in *Scenes from the Heroic Life*, by Carl Sternheim. I have slightly revised Brown's translation.

    2. For Molière's influence on Sternheim cf. chapter 6 of this study.

    3. This is the conclusion reached by most critics. Even Wilhelm Emrich, who generally follows Sternheim's own interpretations and emphasizes the positive qualities of his heroes, describes Schippel's actions as a result of "instinctive and blind adaptation!" (*Gesamtwerk*, 1:16). Cf. also M. Linke, *Sternheim*, p. 74.

    4. The following interpretation of the text is also confirmed by the early versions of this comedy where Schippel is still given the opportunity to explain his intentions and strategies in several soliloquies (cf. *Gesamtwerk*, vol. 10, pt. 2, pp. 796–897).

    5. Within the terms of the representational games, ridicule is of course the punishment which awaits any hero who does not succeed in impressing others. It is the typical trauma of the social climber and is presented as such both in this and the following play.

    6. Quotations from the text follow the translation of the play by J. M. Ritchie and J. D. Powell in *Scenes from the Heroic Life* by Carl Sternheim.

    7. Cf. chapter 4, note 11.

    8. Cf. chapter 1 of this study.

    9. Cf. Sternheim's early poem "Original at any cost" (*Gesamtwerk*, 9:24). Here as in other places where Sternheim demands that every individ-

ual cultivate a distinguishing attitude, a "nuance," he shows no interest in the content of this sign. Important, however, is the individual's determination to express that which he has chosen as his specific character.

10. Silvio Vietta (in Vietta and Kemper, *Expressionismus*, p. 102) has interpreted this transaction in the following way: Christian Maske constitutes himself as a "subject" in the sense of Descartes', Fichte's, and Hegel's philosophy, not however through a "process of thinking," but through a "purchasing act," thus becoming a "capitalist monad." This amusing interpretation misses the point that Christian balances his accounts not in order to enter the world of capitalistic business, but in order to constitute himself as a quasi-aristocratic public person.

11. For Sternheim's radical aversions against the moderate policies of the Social Democratic party cf. his comedy *Tabula Rasa*. For an interpretation of this scene, from the point of view of a Social Democratic critic, cf. B. Diebold, (*Anarchie*, p. 104) who reads Sybil's words as signifying the author's own return to morality.

Chapter Six

1. For the relationship between changes in social reality and innovations in dramatic technique cf. Peter Szondi, *Theorie des modernen Dramas* (Frankfurt, 1956).

2. "Zustand" (1914), in *Gesamtwerk*, 6:22.

3. "Das gerettete Bürgertum" (1918), in *Gesamtwerk*, 6:22.

4. This is also an eminent principle of comedy, which tends to protest against, and reduce, idealizations and abstractions in favor of that which is immediately accessible to the senses.

5. Cf. *Gesamtwerk*, vol. 10, pt. 2, pp. 796–898.

6. This is true for certain scenes in Sternheim's comedies (for instance, the scenes of the second act of *The Bloomers*); it is also true for the grand gestures with which Sternheim's heroes stage their characters and their emotions.

7. Cf. Franz Blei, *Über Wedekind, Sternheim und das Theater* (Leipzig, 1915), and Otto Mann, "Carl Sternheim: Bürger Schippel," in *Das deutsche Drama*, ed. Benno von Wiese (Düsseldorf, 1958), 2:286.

8. In the second edition of *The Strongbox* (1926), Sternheim emphasized these elements of antiexpressionist parody. They are, however, already noticeable in the first edition of the play.

9. For the use of this technique cf. above all *The Bloomers*, act 3 and act 4, scene 8 and the confrontations between Elsbeth and Krull in *The Strongbox*.

10. Cf. *Gesamtwerk*, 6:38.

11. "'My life is about to take a completely new turn" (*R*, 158); "One must be older than you to discern the core of a relationship between man and man. Let's keep to what's visible" (*S*, 147); "You were foaming at the mouth"(*S*, 154).

12. "Molière der Bürger" (1912), in *Gesamtwerk*, 6:17.

13. A study of the reception of Molière's plays in Germany does not yet exist. It can only be suggested, therefore, that this rather uncommon interpretation is indebted to Franz Blei.

14. For the political importance of the representational arts in seventeenth-century society cf. Norbert Elias, *Die höfische Gesellschaft* (Neuwied: Luchterhand, 1969).

15. Indicative in this respect are titles such as "Molière der Bürger" or "Das gerettete Bürgertum."

16. "Molière" (1917), in *Gesamtwerk*, 6:28–31.

17. For Sternheim's opposition to the eighteenth- and nineteenth-century tradition of tragedy cf. *Gesamtwerk*, 6:537–65.

18. *Gesamtwerk*, 6:19: The dramatic poet "kann die moribunde Eigenschaft in den Helden selbst senken und ihn mit fanatischer Eigenschaft von ihr besessen sein lassen (Wesen der Komödie)." This sentence has been quoted by numerous critics as an argument in favor of a satirical reading of Sternheim's comedies. To make their point, these critics read the term "moribund" as "causing death." Obviously, however, a moribund quality is one which is threatened with extinction. Hence, in Sternheim's terms, the "homeopathic" approach of the comic playwright, who tries to keep such "moribund" qualities alive by presenting heroes who are "possessed with them."

19. It needs to be stressed at this point that early twentieth-century German aesthetic theories tend to discern only two variants of the comic: the satirical and the humorous. This limited notion of comedy is still noticeable in present-day discussions both on comedy in general and on Sternheim in particular. For the history of the theory of the comic in Germany cf. Georgina Baum, *Humor und Satire in der bürgerlichen Ästhetik* (Berlin, 1959).

20. Cf., for instance, Paul Rilla, *Essays,* pp. 202–9, and Wolfgang Gersch, "Diagnose des Zerfalls," *Neue deutsche Literatur* 11, no. 8 (August 1963): 202–7.

21. Hans Kaufmann, p. 292.

22. What Sternheim calls a "truly personal character" can refer to a human individual, to a social class, to a geographical region, or to a histori-

cal period; in other words, it can refer both to individual and to collective phenomena.

23. Cf. Karasek, p. 37.

24. In later years, when Sternheim became a radical critic of the middle class, he himself emphasized this specific function of ideologies in modern capitalistic societies. Cf. his essay "The German Revolution," in *Gesamtwerk*, 6:71–86.

25. For this aspect of Sternheim's work cf. my article "Zum Verhältnis von Politik und Ästhetik bei Carl Sternheim," in *Carl Sternheim*, ed. Wolfgang Wendler (Neuwied, 1980).

Chapter Seven

1. The quotations from the text are taken from *1913*, trans. J. M. Ritchie, in *Scenes from the Heroic Life of the Middle Classes*, by Carl Sternheim.

2. Cf. Autorenkollektiv, *Geschichte der deutschen Literatur*, vol. 9, ed. Hans Kaufmann, (Berlin, 1974), p. 495.

3. Cf. Manfred Linke, *Sternheim*, pp. 81–88.

4. Cf. Christian's statements on economic policies at the end of *The Snob*.

5. *Gesamtwerk*, 7:686.

6. Cf. Sternheim's wartime commentaries on expressionist writers in *Gesamtwerk*, 6:21, 32–38, 200.

7. The unconvincing allegory, used in this scene, made some later critics wonder whether Sternheim had intended a positive or a satirical intepretation of the character of Friedrich Stadler. Cf. Karasek, p. 45.

8. The example is taken from Robert R. Heitner, *German Tragedy in the Age of Enlightenment* (Berkeley: University of California Press, 1963), p. 7.

9. Quotations from the text refer to *Gesamtwerk*, vol. 2. The translations are mine. In some parts, the interpretation of the play is indebted to Franz Norbert Mennemeyer, "Carl Sternheims Komödie der Politik," *Deutsche Vierteljahrsschrift für Literaturwissenschaft und Geistesgeschichte* 44 (1970): 705–26.

10. In this respect, Ständer is the first example of a comic hero who follows the example of Molière's *Misanthrope* or, at least, Sternheim's interpretation thereof (cf. *Gesamtwerk*, 6:17).

11. In this comedy, as well as in others, the evaluation of the central figure is the most controversial point. Most comtemporary critics consid-

ered Ständer either a political parasite (Diebold, p. 100) or a representative of some moderate political party (Harry Graf Kessler, *Tagebücher 1918–1937*, ed. Wolfgang Pfeiffer-Belli (Frankfurt: Insel, 1961), p. 120, and Siegfried Jacobsohn, "Tabula Rasa," *Das Jahr der Bühne* 7 (1917–18): 184). In addition, practically all critics emphasized Sternheim's unequivocally negative and satirical treatment of Ständer. The author himself suggested three somewhat contradictory interpretations of his hero. Until the end of the war, he presented him as a positive middle-class hero (*Gesamtwerk* 6:59); during the years of the German revolution (November 1918–20), he sided with Sturm against Ständer, who was now seen as an example of a proletarian turned bourgeois (*Gesamtwerk*, 6:81, 148); in later years he praised him as an embodiment of human emancipation, as a hero who "embarks toward a higher realm of social freedom" (*Gesamtwerk*, 6:208, 221). Such evaluative differences reflect Sternheim's changing political opinions and, above all, his temporary sympathies for leftist radical positions (cf. chapter 9 of this study).

12. Cf. Mennemeyer, "Sternheims Komödie," p. 732, and Jörg Schönert, "Zur Textanalyse von Sternheims Dramen," pp. 76–81.

13. For the use of this image among anarchist writers cf. Siegfried Landauer, *Erkenntnis und Befreiung*, ed. R. Link-Salinger (Frankfurt: Suhrkamp, 1976), p. 16.

14. A seventeenth-century, comedy figure whose name was derived from the English "bosset," "beer." Cf. Heinz Kindermann, *Theatergeschichte Europas*, vol. 3 (Salzburg: Otto Müller, 1969), p. 353.

15. Hegel, *Ästhetik* 2:571.

16. Jean Jacques Rousseau, "Lettre à M. D'Alembert," in *Oeuvres Complètes* (Paris: Dalibon, 1824), 2:200–202.

17. Michail Bachtin, *Literatur und Karneval: Zur Romantheorie und Lachkultur*, trans. Alexander Kämpfe (Munich: Hanser, 1969). A similar attempt at reviving the "Dionysian tradition" is found in Salomon Friedländer, *Schöpferische Indifferenze*, 2d ed. (Munich: F. Reinhardt, 1926), p. xviii.

18. *Gesamtwerk*, 6:125.

Chapter Eight

1. Sternheim's presentation of reality in the form of an energy system may be indebted to Nietzsche who, in some parts of his work, interprets natural events and human activities as an exchange between "stimuli of energy" ("Kraftauslösungen") and concludes that actions which are normally thought to be guided by some goal or purpose are, in reality, a "sudden ex-

plosion of power" (Friedrich Nietzsche, *Werke*, vol. 13 [Leipzig: C. G. Neumann, 1903], p. 263). Instead of paying attention to the entirety of Sternheim's metaphorical system, the overwhelming majority of critics have considered his novellas separate entities and prime examples of either a grotesque or a satirical mode of expressionist narration. Notable exceptions to this general tendency are Inge Jens, "Studien zur Entwicklung der expressionistischen Novelle" (Ph.D. Diss., University of Tübingen, 1953) and Wolfgang Wendler, *Carl Sternheim*. For Sternheim's influence on expressionist narrative prose cf. Armin Arnold, *Prose des Expressionismus* (Stuttgart: Kohlhammer, 1972).

2. In all but three cases Sternheim's novellas are named after their central figures. It is, therefore, generally unnecessary to indicate the titles of the novellas separately. Stefanie—one of the exceptions—is the heroine of the novella *Die Poularde*.

3. The name is a rather obvious allusion to the poet Rainer Maria Rilke, friend of Marie Fürstin von Thurn und Taxis.

4. Cf. for instance the interpretations given in Vietta and Kemper, *Expressionismus*, pp. 100–10.

5. Cf. the above interpretation of *1913*.

6. For the continuity of such metaphors in Sternheim's works cf. chapter 1, section 4 and chapter 2 of this study.

7. Sternheim's identification with Büchner is even more noticeable in the manuscript of "Tasso" where the author speaks of Büchner's—and Grabbe's—"heisses Liebesbekenntnis zu unbegrenzter Lebensfülle" (*Gesamtwerk*, 6:551). Such interpretations, one can add, do justice to at least some central intentions of Büchner's works. Cf. Thomas Michael Mayer, "Büchner und Weidig," in *Text und Kritik, Sonderband Georg Büchner* (Munich: Text und Kritik, 1979), pp. 84–86.

8. Cf. Hellmuth Himmel, *Geschichte der deutschen Novelle* (Berne: Francke, 1964), pp. 415–27: Colette Dimić, "Das Groteske in der Erzählung des Expressionismus" (Ph.D. diss., University of Tübingen, 1970); Herbert Kraft, *Kunst und Wirklichkeit im Expressionismus* (Bebenhausen: Rotsch, 1972); and Fritz Martini, "Einleitung," in his anthology *Prosa des Expressionismus* (Stuttgart: Reclam, 1977).

9. Cf. *Gesamtwerk*, 6:21.

10. Cf. Henri Bergson, especially his major work *L'Evolution Créatrice*.

11. This concept is central to the German current of *Lebensphilosophie*, above all to the works of Wilhelm Dilthey and Georg Simmel.

12. Sternheim had befriended Benn in Brussels in 1917. Benn's influence on Sternheim, manifest both on the thematic and the stylistic levels, requires a separate study.

13. For the relationship between Edschmid and Sternheim cf. *Gesamt-werk*, 6:530, and Kasimir Edschmid, *Lebendiger Expressionismus* (Munich: Desch, 1961).

14. Cf. *Gesamtwerk*, 4:430–35. A later critic, Ernst Sebald, has compiled an impressive list of the sexual images and episodes in Sternheim's works. Sebald argues that Sternheim, like many Wilhelminian males, suffered from an oral fixation and indulged in violent sexual dreams. While it is true that scenes describing violent sexual acts occur frequently in Sternheim's prose, it must be emphasized that they do not necessarily express the author's "subconscious wishes." In most cases they should be read as descriptions and denunciations of the exploitative character of existing human relationships.

15. This is true for the novellas *Meta, Ulrike*, and *Posinsky*.

16. For a similar explanation of impressionism cf. Heinrich Vogler, *Proletkult* (Hanover: Paul Steegemann, 1920), p. 7.

Chapter Nine

1. Cf. Manfred Linke, pp. 90–95.

2. Above all *Der Kandidat* (1914, an adaption of Flaubert's play); *Der Scharmante* (1915, a play based on Guy de Maupassant's *La paix du ménage*); a readaptation of Friedrich Maximilian Klinger's play *Das leidende Weib* (1915); a modernized translation of Molière's play *L'Avare* (1917); *Die Marquise von Arcis* (1918, based on an episode from Diderot's novel *Jacques le Fataliste et son maître*).

3. Cf. *Gesamtwerk*, 6:420. For the hostilities between Sternheim and his critics cf. also Kurt Pinthus, "Carl Sternheim," *Der Querschnitt* 5 (1925): 593–96.

4. *Gesamtwerk*, 1:307.

5. Franz Blei, *Erzählung eines Lebens* p. 437; "Der Umschlag in die fast nur mehr parteipolitisch bestimmte Aggression des 'bürgerlichen Helden' kam, als Sternheim vom Krieg und seinem Verlauf merkte, dass die Pädagogik, die er bis 1914 an den deutschen Bürger gewandt hatte, aussenpolitisch und militärisch vergeblich gewesen war." Two reactions to this insight into the futility of his pedagogical attempts can be distinguished. During a limited period, above all in 1919 and 1920, Sternheim intepreted his bourgeois heroes as representatives of a social system destined to perish. The Maske trilogy thus becomes the dramatic equivalent of Heinrich Mann's novel *Der Untertan*, an equation suggested by Gottfried Benn (Cf. *Gesamtwerk*, 6:167, and Gottfried Benn, "Das moderne Ich," in his *Gesammelte Werke*, ed. D. Wellershoff [Wiesbaden: Limes, 1959], 1:9.)

In later years Sternheim tends to interpret his middle-class heroes as examples of the "anti-authoritarian individual" and their actions as rebellions against social constraints. This latter interpretation follows the model of Sternheim's evaluation of Molière's *Misanthrope* in his first essay on Molière (1912; *Gesamtwerk*, 6:17).

6. The hero of Sternheim's earlier play is, by contrast, modeled on the "senex" figures of the comedy tradition.

7. Cf. Karl Vietor, "Carl Sternheim," *Neue Blätter für Kunst und Literatur* 2, no. 7 (1920): 118–21, and Bernhard Diebold, *Anarchie* p. 120. For a more recent interpretation of Sternheim's "romanticizing turn" cf. Ansgar Hillach, "Die Schule von Uznach oder der 'romantische' Sternheim," *Jahrbuch der deutschen Schillergesellschaft* 15 (1971): 441–64.

8. Cf. Pinthus, "Sternheim."

9. For an interpretation of Pfemfert's position within radical circles of the Weimar Republic cf. Hans Martin Bock, *Geschichte des 'linken Radikalismus' in Deutschland* (Frankfurt, 1976). Sternheim's contributions to *Die Aktion* have been evaluated by Hans Lothar Peter, *Literarische Intelligenz und Klassenkampf*.

10. Cf. Bock, p. 102.

11. Pfemfert was allied with George Grosz and Carl Einstein, who were among the leading figures of the Berlin dada movement. *Die Aktion* played a leading part in the so-called Kunst Lump debate in which reverence toward the bourgeois traditions of art and literature was denounced as counterrevolutionary. Cf. Walter Fähnders and Martin Rector, *Linksradikalismus und Literatur* (Reinbek, 1974), 1:100–107.

12. Among those mentioned are Heine, Wilhelm Weitling, Max Stirner, Proudhon, and Bakunin. Sternheim also refers frequently to such representatives of the Enlightenment as Lessing, Voltaire, Diderot, Baumarchais, and Mirabeau and to such "modernist" artists as Flaubert, Baudelaire, Oscar Wilde, van Gogh, and Gottfried Benn.

13. Cf. "Tasso oder Kunst des Juste Milieu," in *Gesamtwerk*, 6:177–202.

14. Cf. *Gesamtwerk*, 6:50, 89, 98.

15. Sternheim's statements are somewhat ambiguous in this respect. On the one hand, he advises the workers to shun the consumers' goods offered by the bourgeoisie, on the other he denounces asceticism as an element of bourgeois ideology.

16. Cf. *Gesamtwerk*, 6:32–38.

17. Cf. his "Brief an Generaloberst von Seeckt," in *Gesamtwerk*, 6:363. Cf. also Klaus Mann, *Der Wendepunkt: Ein Lebensbericht* (Frankfurt: S. Fischer, 1952), pp. 251–53.

18. Two further plays, "John Pierpont Morgan" and "Aut Caesar aut nihil," were never staged.

19. In this connection the term "Vision" becomes peculiarly important for Sternheim's thinking. Cf. *Gesamtwerk*, 6:182, 193, 196.

20. *Gesamtwerk*, 6:113, 183, 195.

21. *Gesamtwerk*, 6:201.

22. For such thoughts cf. also Sternheim's novel *Europa* (*Gesamtwerk*, 5:194, 177).

23. *Gesamtwerk*, 6:125.

24. *Gesamtwerk*, 6:91.

25. Cf. "Arbeiter ABC" (*Gesamtwerk*, 6:245, 247) and "Hand weg von Margarine!" (*Gesamtwerk*, 6:228).

26. Sternheim makes frequent use of this metaphor in order to characterize his own prewar plays. Cf. *Gesamtwerk*, 6:48, 88, 160, 277, 311.

27. Cf. above all *Gesamtwerk*, 5:303, 313.

28. Cf. the review of the play by Max Hermann-Neisse in *Die Aktion* 14, nos. 2–4 (1924): 89–90.

29. Cf. a similar scene in Sternheim's *Don Juan* (*Gesamtwerk*, 7:514).

30. An explanation of this dialogue, in which the various concepts of water are tied to the consciousness of various social classes, is found in Sternheim's essays "Berlin oder Juste Milieu" (*Gesamtwerk*, 6:169) and "Arbeiter ABC" (*Gesamtwerk*, 6:242). The translations from the *The Fossil* are from Carl Sternheim, *Scenes from the Heroic Life of the Middle Classes*, ed. J. M. Ritchie, cited in the text as *R*.

31. *Gesamtwerk*, 7:689. The quotation is taken from Gottfried Benn's one-act drama "Ithaka."

32. One might say that all those critics who read Sternheim's prewar comedies as fictitious sociological models (Schönert, "Zur Textanalyze") stress the "new objectivity" aspect of these plays.

33. *Gesamtwerk*, 7:687.

34. For a similar interpretation cf. Ansgar Hillach, "Die Schule von Uznach."

35. In Sternheim's drama "John Pierpont Morgan" (1930), one can find a comparable constellation. There the hero, after having visited all the European countries, finally opts for a woman from the provincial town of Oldenburg.

36. *Gesamtwerk*, 3:421.

Selected Bibliography

PRIMARY SOURCES

"Sternheim, Carl. Briefe an Franz Blei." Edited by Rudolf Biletta. *Neue Deutsche Hefte* 18, No. 3 (1971): 36–39.

Gesamtwerk. 10 vols. Edited by Wilhelm Emrich. Neuwied: Luchterhand, 1963–76.

Scenes from the Heroic Life of the Middle Classes: Five Plays. Translated by M. A. L. Brown et al. Edited by J. M. Ritchie. London: Calder and Boyers, 1970.

The Strongbox. Translated by Maurice Edwards and Valerie Reich. In *Anthology of German Expressionist Drama*, edited by Walter H. Sokel. New York: Doubleday, 1963, pp. 90–157.

SECONDARY SOURCES

1. Bibliography

Biletta, Rudolf. *Sternheim-Kompendium*. Wiesbaden: Franz Steiner, 1975. An annotated bibliography listing all the publications of Sternheim's works and all secondary sources (including newspaper articles) up to 1974.

2. Books and Parts of Books

Autorenkollektiv. *Geschichte der deutschen Literatur*. Vol. 9. Edited by Hans Kaufmann. Berlin: Volk und Wissen, 1974. Part of a ten-volume history of German literature covering the years from 1890 to 1917. Writing from a Marxist point of view, the authors stress the realism and the social criticism of Sternheim's comedies.

Baum, Georgina. *Humor und Satire in der bürgerlichen Ästhetik*. Berlin: Aufbau-Verlag, 1959. A study dealing with nineteenth- and twentieth-century aesthetic theories in respect to their treatment of the comic, the humorous, and the satirical. Although an excellent survey, the author tends to equate comedy and satire.

Bayerdörffer, Hans-Peter. "Sternheim: *Die Kassette.*" In *Die deutsche Komödie: Vom Mittelalter bis zur Gegenwart*, edited by Walter Hinck. Düsseldorf: A. Bagel, 1972, pp. 213–32. A interesting interpretation of Sternheim's *The Strongbox* which stresses—and over-emphasizes—the tragic elements of the play.

Blei, Franz. *Über Wedekind, Sternheim und das Theater.* Leipzig: Kurt Wolff, 1915. The first book-length study of Sternheim. Blei, Sternheim's closest friend in the years before World War I, praises Sternheim for freeing comedy from middle-class sentimentalism and for rediscovering the true potential of the genre.

Bock, Hans Martin. *Geschichte des "linken Radiakalismus" in Deutschland.* Frankfurt: Suhrkamp, 1976. An historical survey of left-wing radicalism in Germany from the 1890s to the 1960s.

Dedner, Burghard. "Zum Verhältnis von Politik und Ästhetik bei Carl Sternheim. In *Carl Sternheim*, edited by Wolfgang Wendler. Darmstadt: Luchterhand, 1980. An attempt at tracing Sternheim's political thoughts from the early work *Don Juan* to his break with *Die Aktion* in 1925.

Denkler, Horst. *Das Drama des Expressionismus.* Munich: Fink, 1967. One of the most thorough studies of expressionist drama. Sternheim is grouped with those expressionist dramatists who wrote plays prior to developing specifically "expressionist" theories or programs.

Diebold, Bernhard. *Anarchie im Drama.* 4th ed. Berlin: H. Keller, 1928. A survey of expressionist drama by one of the most prominent theater critics of the period. Diebold is especially critical of Sternheim's postwar plays.

Durzak, Manfred. *Das expressionistische Drama.* Vol. 1. *Carl Sternheim und Georg Kaiser.* Munich: Nymphenburger, 1978. A "middle of the road" interpretation of Sternheim's works. Useful as an introduction.

Emrich, Wilhelm. "Die Komödien Carl Sternheims." In *Der Deutsche Expressionismus*, edited by Hans Steffen. Göttingen: Vandenhoeck und Ruprecht, 1966, pp. 115–37. A major contribution by the editor of Sternheim's works. This article initiated a new approach to Sternheim. Emrich dismisses the satirical interpretation and praises Sternheim as a prophet of individualism.

Fähnders, Walter, and Rector, Martin. *Linksradikalismus und Literatur.* 2 vols. Reinbek: Rowohlt, 1974. The most extensive and thorough study available on the literary theories and debates of left-wing groups in postrevolutionary Germany.

Freund, Winfried. *Die Bürgerkomödien Carl Sternheims*. Munich: Fink, 1976. A study of Sternheim's comedies which stresses the phenomenological and realistic intentions of Sternheim's plays. While giving good interpretations of particular dramatic scenes, the book pays little attention to the historical development of Sternheim's writings.

Hagedorn, Klaus. "Carl Sternheim: Die Bühnengeschichte seiner Dramatik," Ph.D. dissertation, University of Cologne, 1963. A survey of the theatrical productions of Sternheim's plays. Valuable for its documentation of the reception of Sternheim's works.

Hohendahl, Peter Uwe. *Das Bild der bürgerlichen Welt im expressionistischen Drama*. Heidelberg: Winter, 1967. A useful and thorough study of the treatment of the middle classes in German expressionist drama. Hohendahl distinguishes between Sternheim's portrayal of the small world of the philistine in his first plays and his later attack on bourgeois society in general.

Karasek, Hellmuth. *Carl Sternheim*. Velber: Friedrich, 1965. Good, short summaries of Sternheim's plays, stressing their satirical aspects. Very useful as an introduction.

Linke, Manfred. *Carl Sternheim*. Reinbek: Rowohlt, 1979. The only available monograph on Sternheim. Valuable for its biographical information.

Mann, Otto. *Der Dandy*. 2d ed. Heidelberg: Rothe, 1962. A historical study of the dandy in nineteenth-century Europe.

————. "Carl Sternheim: *Bürger Schippel*." In *Das deutsche Drama*, edited by Benno von Wiese. Düsseldorf: A. Bagel, 1958, 2:284–304. Mann interprets Sternheim's play within the tradition of European comedy and, especially, in the light of the Greek prototype of the genre.

Marcuse, Ludwig. "Das Expressionistische Drama." In *Literaturgeschichte der Gegenwart*, edited by Ludwig Marcuse. Vol. 2. Leipzig: F. Schneider, 1925. One of the most interesting contemporary interpretations of Sternheim's plays. According to Marcuse, Sternheim creates the "superbourgeois" by glorifying the philistine.

Paulsen, Wolfgang. *Expressionismus und Aktivismus: Eine typologische Untersuchung*. Berne: Gotthelf, 1935. An early study of German literature between 1910 and 1920. Paulsen distinguishes between the expressionists and the politically engaged "activists." He groups Sternheim among the latter.

————. "Sternheim und die Komödie des Expressionismus." In *Die deutsche Komödie im 20. Jahrhundert*, edited by W. Paulsen. Heidel-

berg: Lothar Stiehm, 1976. The article places Sternheim in the tradition of nineteenth-century realism. Paulsen attempts, at the same
time, a psychological explanation of Sternheim's plays.

Peter, Hans-Lothar. *Literarische Intelligenz und Klassenkampf: Die Aktion
1911–1932*. Cologne: Pahl-Rugenstein, 1972. A study of the journal *Die Aktion*. Sternheim's contributions to the journal are discussed
(and dismissed) from a Marxist point of view.

Reichart, Herbert W. "Nietzsche und Carl Sternheim." In *Nietzsche und
die deutsche Literatur*, edited by Bruno Hillebrand. Tübingen:
Niemeyer, 1978, 2:11–35. An analysis of Nietzsche's influence on
Sternheim. The only treatment of this subject.

Schönert, Jörg. "Zur Textanalyse von Sternheims Dramen: Modell-
struktur und Thesenstruktur." In *Carl Sternheims Dramen*, edited by
Jörg Schönert. Heidelberg: Quelle & Meyer, 1975. An interesting
attempt at distinguishing various stages in Sternheim's dramatic
production. Schönert points to the break between Sternheim's prewar comedies and his later *pièces à thèse*.

Sebald, Winfried Georg. *Carl Sternheim: Kritiker und Opfer der Wilhelminischen Ära*. Stuttgart: Kolhammer, 1969. A socio-psychological
study of Sternheim. Sebald treats Sternheim's prose as an expression
of neurotic symptoms prevalent at the time. Stimulating, though
not always convincing.

Sokel, Walter H. *The Writer in Extremis*. New York: McGraw-Hill,
1964. A study of German expressionist literature. Sternheim is
placed in the vicinity of the painter George Grosz and considered a
forerunner of Bertolt Brecht. Sokel emphasizes the intellectual qualities of Sternheim's writings.

Szondi, Peter. *Theorie des modernen Dramas*. Frankfurt: Suhrkamp, 1956.
A "classic" on the structural characteristics of twentieth-century
drama.

Vietta, Silvio, and Kemper, Hans Georg. *Expressionismus*. Munich: W.
Fink, 1975. The authors stress the nihilistic aspects of expressionist
literature. Sternheim is discussed together with such writers as
Georg Trakl and Franz Kafka.

Wendler, Wolfgang. *Carl Sternheim: Weltvorstellung und Kunstprinzipien*.
Frankfurt: Athenäum, 1966. The first scholarly study of Sternheim's literary intentions and prose works. Still indispensable for an
understanding of his work.

———. "Sternheims Wirklichkeit." In *Carl Sternheim*, edited by Wolfgang Wendler. Darmstadt: Luchterhand, 1980. Wendler explores

the Oedipal theme in Sternheim's oeuvre and thus succeeds in shedding new light on a number of Sternheim's works.

3. Articles

Hillach, Ansgar. "Die Schule von Uznach oder der 'romantische' Sternheim." *Jahrbuch der deutschen Schillergesellschaft* 15 (1971): 441–64. This article gives a detailed analysis of *Uznach School* and discusses the problem of Sternheim's so-called romanticizing turn.

Mennemeyer, Franz Norbert. "Carl Sternheims Komödie der Politik." *Deutsche Vierteljahresschrift für Literaturwissenschaft und Geistesgeschichte* 44 (1970): 705–26. A thorough analysis of Sternheim's political comedy *Tabula Rasa*. Mennemeyer discusses the play in terms of its comic elements and of Sternheim's political position.

Myers, David. "Carl Sternheim: Satirist or Creator of Modern Heroes." *Monatshefte* 65 (1973): 39–47. Myers points at the contradictions between Sternheim's plays and his statements of intent. He interprets Sternheim's heroes as caricatures of middle-class instincts.

Williams, Rhys W. "Carl Sternheim's Image of Marx and his Critique of the German Intellectual Tradition." *German Life and Letters*, n.s. 32 (1978): 19–29. A study of Sternheim's position vis-à-vis Marxism. Williams also points to some hitherto unknown sources from which Sternheim borrowed in his essays and in his novel *Europa*.

Index